THE FOOD & COOKING OF
GERMANY

THE FOOD & COOKING OF
GERMANY

TRADITIONS • INGREDIENTS • TASTES • 60 RECIPES • 300 PHOTOGRAPHS

MIRKO TRENKNER
PHOTOGRAPHS BY JON WHITAKER

aquamarine

This edition is published by Aquamarine, an imprint of Anness Publishing Ltd, Hermes House, 88–89 Blackfriars Road, London SE1 8HA; tel. 020 7401 2077; fax 020 7633 9499

www.aquamarinebooks.com; www.annesspublishing.com

If you like the images in this book and would like to investigate using them for publishing, promotions or advertising, please visit our website www.practicalpictures.com for more information.

UK agent: The Manning Partnership Ltd; tel. 01225 478444; fax 01225 478440; sales@manning-partnership.co.uk
UK distributor: Grantham Book Services Ltd; tel. 01476 541080; fax 01476 541061; orders@gbs.tbs-ltd.co.uk
North American agent/distributor: National Book Network; tel. 301 459 3366; fax 301 429 5746; www.nbnbooks.com
Australian agent/distributor: Pan Macmillan Australia; tel. 1300 135 113; fax 1300 135 103; customer.service@macmillan.com.au
New Zealand agent/distributor: David Bateman Ltd; tel. (09) 415 7664; fax (09) 415 8892

Publisher: Joanna Lorenz
Editorial Director: Helen Sudell
Executive Editor: Joanne Rippin
Designer: Adelle Morris
Photography: Jon Whitaker
Food Stylist: Fergal Connelly
Prop Stylist: Penny Markham
Production Controller: Wendy Lawson

ETHICAL TRADING POLICY

Because of our ongoing ecological investment programme, you, as our customer, can have the pleasure and reassurance of knowing that a tree is being cultivated on your behalf to naturally replace the materials used to make the book you are holding. For further information about this scheme, go to www.annesspublishing.com/trees.

NOTES

Bracketed terms are intended for American readers.
For all recipes, quantities are given in both metric and imperial measures and, where appropriate, in standard cups and spoons. Follow one set of measures, but not a mixture, because they are not interchangeable.
Standard spoon and cup measures are level. 1 tsp = 5ml, 1 tbsp = 15ml, 1 cup = 250ml/8fl oz.
Australian standard tablespoons are 20ml. Australian readers should use 3 tsp in place of 1 tbsp for measuring small quantities.
American pints are 16fl oz/2 cups. American readers should use 20fl oz/2.5 cups in place of 1 pint when measuring liquids.
Electric oven temperatures in this book are for conventional ovens. When using a fan oven, the temperature will probably need to be reduced by about 10–20°C/20–40°F. Since ovens vary, you should check with your manufacturer's instruction book for guidance.
The nutritional analysis given for each recipe is calculated per portion (i.e. serving or item), unless otherwise stated. If the recipe gives a range, such as Serves 4–6, then the nutritional analysis will be for the smaller portion size, i.e. 6 servings.
Measurements for sodium do not include salt added to taste.
Medium (US large) eggs are used unless otherwise stated.

Front cover shows Tartare of matjes herring and salmon, for recipe see page 26–7.

PUBLISHER'S NOTE

Although the advice and information in this book are believed to be accurate and true at the time of going to press, neither the authors nor the publisher can accept any legal responsibility or liability for any errors or omissions that may be made.

Contents

Introduction 6

Geography & landscape 8

Festivals & celebrations 10

Food traditions of Germany 12

Classic ingredients 14

Appetizers, salads & soups 18

Snacks & light meals 36

Fish dishes 48

Meat dishes 58

Poultry & game dishes 78

Puddings & desserts 92

Cakes & breads 104

Useful suppliers 126

Index 127

Introduction

German food in the 21st century is much more than the substantial fare of past centuries. Although the classic hearty ingredients, such as sauerkraut, pork knuckle, rye bread and beer, do still feature in many German homes and restaurants, Germany has much more to offer. This book celebrates the high quality and surprising variety of German cuisine, with recipes that transform nourishing, quality ingredients into delicious traditional dishes.

A traditional cuisine

The history of Germany is one of conquest and re-conquest, division and unification. Germany has always played a dominant role in Europe; its central position between the warm south and the cold north has ensured that its influence has been felt since Roman times. This fertile country was briefly part of the Roman Empire, and although in those days the local German diet consisted mainly of meat, root vegetables and mead (a strongly alcoholic brew based on honey), the influence of a lighter Roman cuisine was soon adopted. Even 2,000 years ago, the countryside provided pasture

Above: The beautiful farms and grazing lands of Germany's Black Forest region.

land for all kinds of cattle, sheep and pigs; grain and vegetables flourished in the fields; and on the warm lower slopes of the hills and mountains, hops and vines were already growing to provide the ubiquitous beer and the light, refreshing wine, such as Riesling, for which Germany is rightly renowned.

Germany has many different kinds of bread, based on all the various grains that can be grown, and mostly still baked using traditional methods. Rye bread is a real favourite, with its dark colour and rich, strong flavour, and is very typical of this part of Europe. Other time-honoured recipes give us the famous German sausages, which use every part of the animal in combination with herbs and spices – a frugal and yet delicious way to preserve meat for the chilly winter. Flavour is added by mixing in spices such as juniper berries, mustard and horseradish.

Dairy products, too, are still made in the old way, with all kinds of cheese, butter, yogurt, milk and soured milk products, all of which are very popular as part of the daily diet. Milk products have a key role in the German food market. There are delicious cheeses made from cow's milk, as well as goat's

Below: The Mosel vineyards and the imposing Landshut Fortress of Bernkastel.

and sheep's milk from every region of the country – more than 500 different kinds are still sold. As with sausages, bread and beer, every region has its own speciality.

Since the 18th century, when King Frederick the Great introduced potatoes to Germany, these humble roots have become a great favourite, and not only as an accompaniment – many recipes for soups, salads and pancakes are based on potato as a main ingredient.

Regional variations

In the 20th century, the differences in the eating habits between the north and south of Germany became more distinctive. The northern, cooler part of the country had a lesser range and quality of products when compared to the south, where the demand for good food and wine was encouraged by its proximity to the gourmet cuisines of Italy and France. Food styles were different too – a heavier cooking style similar to that of Scandinavian food tended to predominate where the winters were

Below: The restaurants of Cologne's old town, near the famous fish market.

Above: Bavarian veal sausage with pretzel and beer, served in Ellmau, Upper Bavaria.

tougher, whereas the warmer areas of the south supported a more varied agriculture, with salad crops and tender vegetables. There was also the division between east and west to consider. The influence of the communist USSR on East Germany led to collective farms, which were not the most productive way to handle agriculture, while West Germany adapted a more flexible and varied way of farming, incorporating ideas from other countries.

Since the reunification of the country in the late 20th century, Germany's cuisine has continued to adapt to outside influences while preserving its strong traditions of excellence. The rustic style of German food has become more sophisticated as restaurants adopt other cooking methods and ingredients, and now Germany can boast some of the best chefs and restaurants in Europe.

The way ahead

Organic and locally produced food have become the focus in Germany in the last few years, as in many other countries. Since the EU brought in a strict labelling scheme in 2001, the consumption of organic products in Germany has grown by about 15 per cent every year. But seasonal and home-grown ingredients have always provided the basis for cooking in Germany, particularly in rural areas, and this is still true today. The emphasis in the 21st century is on improving organic production while maintaining the best of the traditional methods that make German food so delicious.

About this book

This tempting collection of recipes gives an excellent introduction to German cuisine. The first two chapters offer some delicious appetizers and salads, soups full of warming, comforting food for the colder months, and snacks that are suitable for a tasty lunch or a weekday supper. Chapters on fish, meat, poultry and game follow; these are the basis of many German meals. Next comes a chapter full of fabulous desserts, followed by a section on baking, one of the best-loved elements of German cuisine.

Geography & landscape

From the chilly northern sea coast to the warm southern uplands, Germany contains a wide variety of different landscapes. The sea batters the coastline of northern Germany, where the prevailing winds from the west keep the climate moderate all year. Just a few hundred miles further south, the majestic mountains of the Alps have freezing temperatures with snow on the high peaks in winter, but hot summers in the lush valleys down below.

Northern lowlands

Germany has a long and intricate coastline, with the North Sea to the west and the Baltic Sea to the east. The two seas are divided by the Jutland peninsula and the small country of Denmark, which sits in the centre of Germany's northern edge. There is plenty of fish available in these cold, often stormy waters, and much of the food production here is based on fish and shellfish, with traditional ports and fishing villages all along the coast.

The North Sea coastline is famous for its unique mudflats and fertile marshland, where long sand banks help to protect the islands and the mainland from being swamped by storm surges. The everyday life of the people who live

Above: The snowy peaks of Zugspitze, the highest mountain of the Bavarian Alps.

in this area is dominated by the weather and the tides, and it sometimes seems like a land suspended in time.

Further inland, the countryside in this part of Germany is quite flat and low-lying, with wide plains stretching over 100 miles/160 km south to the first range of hills in the centre of the country. As well as being a popular tourist destination, with its expansive landscapes and moderate climate, this part of Germany is ideally suited to agricultural production on a large scale. The winters are comparatively mild,

Left: The shoreline and pier of the Isle of Ruegin, in the often stormy Baltic Sea.

while the summers tend to be quite cool and less sunny than in the hotter, almost Mediterranean south. Many vegetables and cereals are grown here, particularly cabbage, apples, potatoes, wheat and barley.

Central uplands

Further south from the coast, a low mountain range arises that eventually reaches the majestic Danube river in the far south of Germany. Impressive forests still cover many of these mountains, containing abundant wildlife, including game such as deer and wild boar that has traditionally formed part of

Below: Bavarian pastures are ideal for walking and provide lush grazing for cattle.

Above: A local fisherman on Lake Constance displays his catch of perch.

the rural diet. On the sunlit lower slopes, vines, hops and other fruits are grown in great profusion in the sunny, mild climate. The Rhine and Danube rivers and their winding tributaries carve out scenic valleys, some cut so deeply through the rock that before the 20th century communications were almost impossible between villages.

The most attractive areas for tourists are the Harz Mountains and the Schwarzwald (Black Forest), where walking tours are very popular in the summer and cross-country skiing and other snow-based activities in the winter. All these activities work wonders for the appetite, which can be satisfied by a hearty stew and a glass of beer.

Southern hills

Between the Danube and the Alps lie Lake Constance (Bodensee) and the Allgaeu, a picturesque, hilly landscape with forests and meadows. The climate in this area of Germany is very mild, nearly Mediterranean, with hot summers and pleasantly cool winters. Many different fruits and vegetables are grown here. Freshwater fish such as trout have traditionally been caught in great abundance in Lake Constance, and because of greater protection from environmental damage in the 21st century, delicious dishes such as freshly caught pan-fried trout are once more on the menu.

South from Munich, a wonderful, green, mountainous landscape spreads out with forests and meadows. From here there are breathtaking views of the Alps as they rise to divide Germany from Switzerland and Austria.

Germany's Alpine region

The highest mountain in the German Alps is the Zugspitze, which is 2,962 metres high (nearly 10,000 feet). High up in these spectacular mountains, very little farming can be done – the terrain is just too inhospitable. Goats and sheep thrive here, though, and farmers use the mountains for pasture, moving their flocks up in the summer to graze in the highest meadows of grass, and back down to the villages in the winter. Dairy products made from goat's and sheep's milk are typical of this area.

Below: The regions of Germany still enjoy and celebrate distinctive food customs, many of which are influenced by their location and climate.

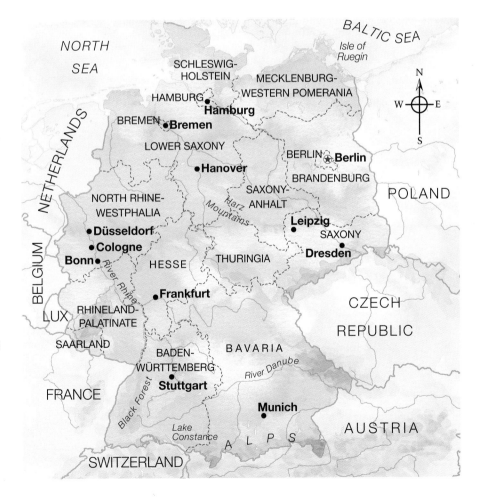

Festivals & celebrations

Germany has a fascinating cultural and religious heritage, and most of the traditional celebrations throughout the year come from its Christian background. Religious rituals are still important, especially in the south of Germany, where most of the people are Catholics. But the overriding factor is the family gathering – for many people this is the most important motive for hosting a special occasion where drinks and good food play a leading role.

New Year's Eve

In the north of Germany there used to be a special tradition of children going from door to door on New Year's Eve, singing to their neighbours in return for sweets and money. Nowadays the singing and sweets are more often found at Halloween, and the most important thing about New Year's Eve is good food and drink, an impressive firework display and a big gathering of friends and family. Favourite dishes for the party include raclette and cheese fondue, both of which originate in Switzerland, and are delicious made with fresh local cheeses. Sometimes there will be a buffet of simpler dishes such as potato salad and frankfurters. For those who have the time and patience to prepare something a little

Above: The decorated top of a maypole, in Viktualienmarkt, Munich.

more elaborate, oven-baked carp with boiled potatoes and cucumber salad is a traditional choice. And for those with a sweet tooth, after midnight, sweet dough dumplings cooked in oil with a marmalade filling are served.

Spring carnivals

In February, carnivals mark the start of Lent, as well as the beginning of spring. In the Rhineland, in particular, the celebrations go on for days, and people join street parades dressed up in fantastic costumes and keep the party going as long as possible. Food is not

Left: Spring carnivals are celebrated with street parades of elaborate costumes.

the main event at these carnivals, but the drinks are another matter! There is no carnival without beer…

Easter

While Christmas is the most important feast in the Protestant north of Germany, Easter takes precedence in the Catholic south. The Christian festival starts on Good Friday and continues until Monday. There are church services on Friday and on Easter Sunday, and after services the family comes together for a special lunch. On Friday it is the custom to eat no meat, so fish dishes are often served, especially roasted carp and pike. For Easter Sunday lunch, the traditional choice is still a roasted lamb joint served with rich gravy, beans and potatoes.

May Day

The ancient festival of 1 May has in modern times become known as Labour Day, but the celebrations have strong links with the past. This joyful holiday is a very strong institution in Germany, and there is much feasting and drinking. On the night of 30 April people go out dancing, and on 1 May, especially in the south, many towns and villages still set up a maypole and gather for traditional music and dancing. One of the most popular foods is a hog roast, cooked in the open air.

Above: Fireworks light up the night sky over Dresden on New Year's Eve.

Summer festivals

During the summer there are many different festivals in town squares and village streets all over the country. The rural regions have the strongest traditions, each bound up with the food of the local area and aimed at bringing the community together to celebrate a good farming year. The biggest and most famous festival is the beer festival in Munich (although it starts in late September it is called the Oktoberfest), which is well known all over the world. Thousands of visitors come every year to have a litre or two of beer and to experience the convivial atmosphere.

3 October

The most important new national holiday in Germany is on 3 October. On this day in 1990 the country became one nation again, after 40 years of separation. The Berlin Wall came down in November 1989, and the following year the governments of East and West Germany confirmed the reunification.

Nowadays, this anniversary is seen as a great excuse for big parties with plenty to eat and drink.

St Nicolas

At the end of November, about a month before Christmas, special Christmas markets are set up in many cities in Germany. The aroma of roasted almonds, candy floss and mulled wine is in the air and people happily wander through the markets, eating nuts and pastries as they go, and lingering over stalls selling everything related to Christmas – food, drink, decorations and presents.

St Nicolas comes to visit Germany on 6 December. Children polish their shoes and put them out by the door overnight – if they behaved well over the last month St Nicolas will fill the shoes with sweets and nuts.

Christmas

The highlight of the winter season is Christmas, a real family occasion. On 24 December Santa Claus will visit, bringing presents for everyone, and

Above: The huge main tent at Oktoberfest, Germany's largest beer festival.

then on Christmas Day itself, the most elaborate dishes are served for dinner. Many Germans love to eat roast duck or goose with dumplings and red cabbage, but game dishes such as venison are also popular.

Below: A typical German Christmas market in Rosenheim, Chiemgau, Bavaria.

Food traditions of Germany

Eating in Germany has changed in the last few decades and home cooking has become more international. Germans have happily adopted ingredients and dishes from other countries, and the resulting fusion dishes are highly successful. In the rural areas of Germany, however, the traditional cuisine still dominates, both in restaurants and in home cooking, and the best of the age-old recipes and methods are maintained with great pride.

Culinary map of Germany

Germany is divided into 16 federal states: ten in the western part of the country and six in the east. These states are quite varied in their landscape, climate and history, with some fascinating culinary traditions linked to the individual characteristics of each state.

In the north, busy ports such as Hamburg have a cosmopolitan feel, with a noticeably international influence on the local cuisine that was established hundreds of years ago. Bremen, Hamburg, Lübeck and

Below: The much-loved German pretzel is eaten at breakfast and lunch to accompany cheeses and cold meats.

Rostock are ancient Hanseatic cities, part of a trading group that dominated the Baltic and North Sea for 400 years. Merchants in these ports dealt in goods from all over the world, including exotic spices, rice, coffee and tea, and this meant that the daily food of people in the northern states was not only based on local produce, but was also enriched by all kinds of exciting tastes from abroad. Another important influence on the cuisine of the north is the sea, which means there is a wide range of seafood on the menu.

The central part of Germany (Brandenburg, North Rhine Westphalia, Saxony-Anhalt, Saxony, Thuringia and Hesse) is home to a really rustic, natural cuisine based on fresh, locally grown staples as well as some more recent imports. Saxony is the place to find the best cakes, gateaux, pastries and a coffee culture with a long tradition.

Berlin, in the north-east of the country, is a city state, the most international town in Germany. As far back as the 17th century, Huguenot refugees from France brought their own ideas of cooking to the area. Today, influences from all over the world create a delicious fusion cuisine in Berlin, with its roots in German traditions.

The south, made up of the states of Rhineland Palatinate, Baden-Württemberg, Saarland and Bavaria,

Above: Sausages are cooked outside in huge quantities for Germany's carnivals.

has the most distinguished regional cuisine. The influence of the bordering countries, France, Switzerland and Austria, brought an interest in the best techniques and finest ingredients to these states. The Bavarians particularly love pork in all its forms – roasted, in stews and soups and of course preserved as sausage. The climate is ideal for vines, and this is the best wine-producing area in Germany.

Modern imports

It is more common to eat out in Germany than it used to be, and restaurants are also becoming much more international. Since the mid-1950s, guest workers have been arriving in Germany from Italy, Yugoslavia, Greece and Turkey. In a few decades, these people have inspired most Germans to embrace foreign food, and today a German city without an Italian or Greek restaurant is unthinkable. Later in the 20th century, Asian, Spanish and Japanese restaurants followed, and these days it is quite common to have sushi or tapas before going out for a German beer.

Because of its political orientation, from 1945 to 1990 West Germany was more influenced by Italian, French and Asian cooking styles, while East Germany adapted some of the food customs of the Eastern bloc from countries such as Poland, Hungary and the USSR. After the Berlin Wall came down, everything went back into the German cooking pot and a happy mixture of styles resulted.

The 'fast food' culture has hit Germany, but it is not only the well-known American hamburger chains that can be found throughout the country: Italian, Asian and Turkish fast food is

Above: Fruit and vegetables are displayed at the outdoor market held in the old town area of Düsseldorf.

equally popular. This has led to some interesting combinations, such as Currywurst mit Pommes (a fried German sausage served with spicy Indian sauce and chips).

No matter how international the country becomes, people in Germany have a deep desire for traditional food. German food is not just habit or routine, it is seen as a central element of an historical inheritance. When families come together for a feast the highlight is always a time-honoured dish such as

lamb at Easter, and goose or duck at Christmas, while true German ingredients, such as pork knuckle, sauerkraut, stollen and gingerbread are embedded in the culinary psyche.

Food throughout the day

Breakfast is an important meal, with a range of different breads and rolls, jam, cheese, sausages, ham and eggs. The main meal of the day used to be lunch, when hot soups, stews and other main courses based on meat or fish were served, plus a dessert; later in the day, dinner would be a cold meal, with bread, salad and again cheese, sausages and ham.

These days the meals are often reversed, with a cold lunch and a hot evening meal, which fits in better with the modern working day. Lunchtime is roughly from 12 to 2pm, and most people eat dinner between 7 and 9pm. People also love to drink coffee or tea in the afternoons, with a slice of gateau.

Above: Germans love cheeses and cold meats, and their delicatessens are full of locally cured hams and pork products.

Classic ingredients

In the 21st century, with excellent transport links and food preservation, all sorts of exciting ingredients are available throughout Germany for 12 months of the year. However, the best cooks still choose local produce in season, harking back to the times when country life was dominated by whatever was available in the fields or the larder, and keeping the ancient farming and cooking traditions alive.

Fish

Sea fish German recipes often use fresh sea fish such as cod, herring and salmon, caught in the cold waters of the North Sea and the Baltic off the northern coast. Herring dishes abound, while Alaskan pollack (coalfish) and tuna are becoming very popular.

Freshwater fish Produce from the many rivers and lakes of Germany features less often than sea fish. One exception is the delicious trout from the fast-flowing streams of the central region. Whole carp and pike are still roasted on special occasions, particularly on Good Friday. Other specialities are perch from Lake Constance and eels from the Moselle.

Preserved fish Smoking is one of the oldest methods of preserving fish, and gives it a unique flavour. The best kinds

Below: Herring, a favourite in the North

Above: Smoked Moray eel fillets

Above: The much-loved pork knuckle

of fish for smoking are those with a high fat content (for example, salmon, trout, moray eels or mackerel). Prawns are also smoked, adding strength to their natural salty flavour. Smoked eel and herring seem to have a particular affinity with Germany's strong-tasting dark rye bread, and make a favourite snack or light lunch. Marinated pickled herring is also very popular in Germany, often swallowed whole and washed down with a glass of beer.

Meat

Pork Every part of the pig is used in German recipes, not just the best cuts. Pork knuckle (Schweinshaxe) is a traditional dish that makes the most of a lesser cut by braising it very slowly and gently until it is mouthwateringly tender. But in Germany pork is most often

found in the form of sausage. This is the best way to preserve meat for eating at any time of year, and arose from the times when fresh meat was simply not available all year round and the housewife had to plan ahead for the cold winter months.

German sausages are nearly all based on pork, with the addition of any amount of different herbs, vegetables, grains and spices; it is said that there are at least 1,500 different varieties. They are eaten on their own (fried, grilled (broiled) or poached), with bread, or added to soups and stews.

Ham Another favourite preserved meat is smoked, dried or cooked ham. Black Forest ham is a typical example of the delicious regional variations still available in Germany, some of which can take months to prepare properly, allowing no

Above: Cured pig cheeks

short cuts. First, the pork meat is cured for two to three weeks in brine with salt, sugar, herbs and spices such as juniper berries, bay leaves, cloves, mustard seeds, coriander seeds and peppercorns. Then the meat is lifted out of the brine and stored for two weeks, then smoked over fir and spruce wood for another few weeks. By now the meat will have developed its dark colour and unique taste. It is kept for two to three weeks longer in cold storage to develop its amazing flavour.

Another favourite cured meat is pig cheeks, full of flavour and very tender.

Other meats The next most popular meat after pork is chicken – another

convenient source of protein found on the family farm – and finally beef. Lamb, venison, hare, duck and goose are all part of German culinary history, but are not really everyday foods; they tend to be cooked as the centrepiece of a special meal such as Easter Sunday lunch or a family birthday.

Dairy products

Milk Cow's milk is by far the most popular, but there is also a market for goat's and sheep's milk, particularly in the south of the country, where goats and sheep are easier to tend in the steep, rocky terrain.

Cheese Many different kinds of cheese play a central role in German meals, for example, strong tasty cheese is an important ingredient in the famous Bavarian snack, Brotzeit, a delicious mixture of cheese, ham and gherkins with full-bodied dark rye bread,

Other dairy products The lush pasture lands of southern Germany are ideal grazing grounds, giving quantities of creamy milk. Sour cream is stirred into soups, and makes a topping for pancakes. Dairy products are also used as a base for desserts that are served with sharp, tangy berries.

Above: Plums, often added to Rumtopf

Fruit

The favourite locally-grown fruit in Germany is the apple, and as apples are available over most of the year they are also the most common. Large apple farms in the 'Alten Land' near Hamburg in the north, and around Lake Constance in the south, produce many delicious varieties. The start of summer brings the berry season, when strawberries are soon followed by raspberries, blueberries, blackberries, red and black currants. Rumtopf, a compote of preserved fruit in alcohol, makes the most of seasonal fruits, resulting in a heady concoction for the cold and dark of the winter months.

Below: The famous Black Forest ham

Below: Soft creamy quark cheese

Below: Sweet black cherries

Rumtopf

Begin making Rumtopf in the summer, and in 2–3 months you can start to enjoy this wonderful fruit compote.

750ml/1¼ pints/3 cups rum

250g/9oz/1¼ cups sugar

5 pieces star anise

3 cinnamon sticks

1 vanilla pod (bean), cut into pieces

500g/1¼lb strawberries, cleaned, hulled and halved

Mix the rum with the sugar and spices and add the strawberries. Put the mixture in a jar, cover and keep it in a cool, dark place. When new fruits are in season (blueberries, cherries, peaches, apricots), clean them, cut them up and add to the container, topping up with more sugar and rum to cover.

Vegetables

Potatoes When potatoes were first introduced from South America 200 years before, they were seen as not much more than food for the pigs. This changed when King Frederick II realized how good they were and encouraged the population to eat them. Now Germans fry, boil and mash potatoes, eat them cold in salad, and form them into dumplings and pancakes.

Brassicas The brassica season lasts the whole year, so these vegetables

Above: White and green asparagus

have always been staple foods in Germany, especially in the north. White and red cabbage, Brussels sprouts, cauliflower, curly kale, kohlrabi, Savoy cabbage and pointed cabbage are widely used raw, cooked or fried; these vegetables are real all-rounders. They crop up in many German recipes, for example in soups, added to meat or game stew, stuffed and rolled with minced (ground) meat, and of course as a hot side vegetable or a cold salad.

Asparagus Every year, depending on the weather, the short asparagus season starts around the end of April, by which time many Germans are already waiting impatiently for the first home-grown asparagus. Although you

Below: Morel mushrooms

Above: Pumpkin, an autumn favourite

can buy imported asparagus the whole year round, it cannot be compared with the first fresh local spears. Germans enjoy both white and green asparagus as a side dish or as the basis for a delicate appetizer, served with smoked fish and a piquant dressing.

Other vegetables There are lots of other vegetables that Germans enjoy. Beetroot (beet) is a special favourite, as are carrots and, in the autumn, squashes such as pumpkin. Germans also have a special love for mushrooms and enjoy hunting for wild ones from late summer through the autumn months. Chanterelles are the most common variety, but the woods are also full of porcini and morels.

Below: Red cabbage

Sauerkraut The best-known German cabbage dish is sauerkraut. Many centuries ago, the Romans used fermentation to preserve fresh cabbage, and now sauerkraut is seen as typical of German cuisine. To make sauerkraut, white cabbage is sliced very finely, mixed with salt, sugar and spices, pounded and then pressed in stoneware pots or a wooden cask for about four weeks to ferment. It is rarely made at home now, and is usually bought bottled or canned.

Flavourings and condiments
German dishes are rarely hot and spicy. Popular herbs are parsley, thyme, laurel, and chives, while the most common spices are black pepper (used in small amounts), juniper berries and caraway. Caraway imparts a warm, gentle flavour and is used in sauerkraut, stews, breads and cheeses. Cardamom, aniseed and cinnamon are used in cakes or beverages associated with Christmas, and sometimes in the preparation of sausages, but are otherwise rare in German meals.

When it comes to condiments, mustard is the German favourite, especially with the beloved sausage. Horseradish is also commonly used, either on its own or enriched with cream. Gherkins – preserved tiny cucumbers – are very popular.

Drinks
Beer All over the world Germany is renowned for its long tradition of high-quality brewing. Since 1516, brewers have conformed to a unique German law requiring that beer is made only of barley malt, hops and water, and absolutely nothing else.

There are more than 5,000 different German beers, brewed by 1,200 different breweries, from the smallest regional firms to big names. However, differences between the north and south are quite noticeable, in the north beer tends to be more dry and bitter, while in the south the taste is mild and malty. Beer drinking traditions are different too: in Cologne and Düsseldorf in the Rhineland, beer is served in small glasses measuring less than half a pint (0.2 litres), whereas in Bavaria it comes in large glasses containing a pint or even two pints (1 litre) at a time.

Wine German white wines have an excellent reputation. Riesling is one of the best in the world, and sweet wines such as Trockenbeerenauslese are perfect for drinking with a dessert.

Spirits Korn, a fierce clear spirit comparable to vodka, is made out of grain or potatoes and is especially popular in the north of the country.

Below: Home-baked rye bread

Above: A glass of German beer

During the autumn season, distillers use fruits to produce many different kinds of schnapps (brandy).

Coffee The large trading port of Hamburg in the far north of Germany is the biggest market for fresh, raw coffee beans in the world, and this means that some of the largest coffee roasting companies are located nearby.

Tea Fresh tea is imported into Germany via the same ports as the coffee beans. In the windswept coastal area of East Friesland, the people drink ten times more tea than other Germans.

Bread
The bakers of Germany prepare a range of over 600 different kinds of bread that are used as the basis for breakfast, snacks, a quick lunch and to accompany the main meal of the day. In fact the German word for snack – Brotzeit – literally means 'bread time'. The fantastic varieties of wholemeal and dark rye breads available include added flavours such as spices, herbs, garlic, onions or cheese.

APPETIZERS, SALADS & SOUPS

Red cabbage salad
with walnuts

Spiced pickled pumpkin

Asparagus and smoked
fish salad

Tartare of matjes herring
and salmon

Rhenish sausage salad
with Emmental

Potato salad with frankfurters

Parsnip soup with Black
Forest ham

Carrot and apple cream soup

Asparagus soup with North
Sea prawns

Potato soup with sausages

Sauerkraut soup with bacon

The perfect way to begin a meal

A range of delicious cold appetizers make a welcome beginning to a German meal. There will usually be a good selection of salads, sausages, cheeses and bread, including fresh and preserved ingredients. In former times it was important to preserve food for the winter in vinegar or oil, or by smoking fish or meat, and of course this is also a great way to add more flavour to the dishes. These days it is easy to mix both fresh and preserved food to create mouthwatering dishes to tempt the palate. The perfect start to the evening would be any one or two of these recipes with a cold beer or a glass of crisp Riesling. They can be made in small portions and served as a kind of German tapas.

Germany has more different kinds of sausage than any other country in the world. Smoked, cooked or even raw sausages are mostly made of pork, and there should be no problem in finding the perfect sausage to go with the chosen vegetables, bread or salad. Fish is another popular ingredient in appetizers, whether fresh or smoked.

In former times, soup was often served as a main dish; nowadays, it is more often found as the introduction to a meal before the main course, a perfect warming appetizer on cold days. The range goes from creamy, light vegetable soups, through strong meat broths, to hearty mixtures that could make a meal in their own right. The best base for every soup is a good stock. If time allows, it is definitely worth making fresh stock. It does not take too much work, but the small amount of extra effort will produce a very well-flavoured dish.

Serves 4

800g/1¾lb red cabbage
30ml/2 tbsp red wine vinegar
10ml/2 tsp sunflower oil
75g/3oz shelled walnuts
20ml/4 tsp apple sauce
5ml/1 tsp cranberry jam
salt, ground white pepper and sugar

Red cabbage salad with walnuts
Rotkohlsalat mit Wallnüssen

A fresh, crunchy salad of raw red cabbage is rich in vitamins and minerals and is particularly good in winter, when fresh vegetables are more limited. You can make the salad with white cabbage too, but use white wine vinegar for the dressing. This is delicious served with slices of smoked duck breast.

1 Trim the red cabbage and slice it finely. Put it in a bowl, season with salt, pepper and sugar, and pour over the vinegar and sunflower oil. Toss the salad thoroughly, using your hands, then place in the refrigerator and chill for at least 3 hours to allow the cabbage to absorb the dressing.

2 Just before serving, heat a frying pan over medium heat and toast the walnuts gently, stirring, for 3–4 minutes, until lightly browned and fragrant.

3 Mix the apple sauce and the cranberry jam, and stir into the cabbage salad. Taste the cabbage and add extra salt, vinegar or sugar as necessary. Turn into a salad bowl and scatter with the toasted walnuts.

Energy 240kcal/991kJ; Protein 5.6g; Carbohydrate 12.4g, of which sugars 12.1g; Fat 18.8g, of which saturates 1.7g; Cholesterol 0mg; Calcium 116mg; Fibre 4.9g; Sodium 16mg

Spiced pickled pumpkin
Im Essig-Gewürzfond marinierter Kürbis

Pickling vegetables is a traditional way to preserve them; in the past the cellar shelves in every German household would have been well stocked with preserving jars. It is important to make this a couple of days ahead so that the pumpkin has time to marinate and absorb the spicy flavours.

1 Put the water and vinegar in a large pan and add the sugar and all the spices. Bring to the boil.

2 Add the sliced pumpkin and onion and simmer for about 5 minutes until the pumpkin is tender, but still has a little bite. Remove from the heat and season with salt and white pepper.

3 Transfer the pumpkin and the liquid to a lidded container and leave it to stand for 1–2 days in the refrigerator. To serve, drain the pumpkin from the liquid and spices and serve with bread. Once opened, store in the refrigerator for up to 2 weeks.

Energy 124kcal/525kJ; Protein 1.4g; Carbohydrate 30.6g, of which sugars 29.5g; Fat 0.3g, of which saturates 0.2g; Cholesterol 0mg; Calcium 61mg; Fibre 1.7g; Sodium 2mg

Serves 4

300ml/½ pint/1¼ cups water

300ml/½ pint/1¼ cups white wine vinegar

300g/11oz/1½ cups sugar

2 bay leaves

2 allspice berries

1 cinnamon stick

2 star anise

1 clove

600g/1lb 6oz pumpkin, seeds removed, thinly sliced or cubed

1 onion, sliced

salt and ground white pepper

fresh mint or parsley, to garnish

Cook's tip The pickling liquid can be kept, chilled, for up to 4 weeks and used for another batch of pumpkin.

Serves 4

600g/1lb 6oz white asparagus, peeled and cut diagonally into 1cm/½in pieces

300g/11oz green asparagus, peeled and sliced as above

20ml/4 tsp sunflower oil

1 onion, finely sliced

15ml/1 tbsp cider vinegar

15ml/1 tbsp apple juice

10 cherry tomatoes, halved

400g/14oz mixed smoked fish (salmon, trout, eel, mackerel or halibut)

salt, ground white pepper, sugar

finely chopped parsley, to garnish

For the sauce

200ml/7fl oz/scant 1 cup yogurt

200ml/7fl oz/scant 1 cup sour cream

5ml/1 tsp medium-hot mustard

juice of ½ lemon

2 hard-boiled eggs, separated into yolk and white

10ml/2 tsp sunflower oil

150g/5oz fresh herbs (chervil, parsley, chives, watercress, sorrel, borage and salad burnet), very finely chopped

salt, ground white pepper, sugar

Asparagus and smoked fish salad
Spargelsalat mit geräuchertem Fisch

A mixture of white and green asparagus with cherry tomatoes makes this a colourful salad with an intense flavour. It is accompanied by Frankfurt green sauce, which is served with many dishes involving fish or pan-fried meat. The classic recipe includes seven different fresh herbs, but if you can't find them all just use larger quantities of the ones you have.

1 Cook the prepared asparagus in separate pans in salted water for 4–5 minutes or until just tender. Drain and refresh under cold running water. The stems should retain a little bite. Put the white asparagus in a bowl and set the green aside.

2 Heat the oil in a frying pan over medium heat and cook the onions for 2 minutes until slightly softened. Then add the vinegar and apple juice and season with salt, pepper and sugar. Bring the mixture to the boil and remove from the heat. Pour the hot dressing over the white asparagus. Stir in the cherry tomatoes and leave the salad to marinate for 1–2 hours.

3 To make the Frankfurt green sauce, mix the yogurt with the sour cream, mustard and lemon juice and season to taste with salt, pepper and sugar.

4 Mash the egg yolk with a fork and blend with the oil, then stir into the yogurt and cream mixture. Finely dice the egg white and stir it into the dressing, together with the chopped herbs.

5 Drain the asparagus and tomatoes from the dressing and toss with the green asparagus and the chopped parsley. Arrange the salad on serving plates, surrounded by the sliced or flaked smoked fish. Serve the sauce on the side.

Energy 644kcal/2664kJ; Protein 34.2g; Carbohydrate 13.4g, of which sugars 12.5g; Fat 50.9g, of which saturates 14.4g; Cholesterol 230mg; Calcium 319mg; Fibre 6.1g; Sodium 864mg

Tartare of matjes herring and salmon
Matjestartar auf Pumpernickel

Matjes, or soused, herring is very popular in Germany, especially in the north. It is always eaten cold, sometimes in conjunction with hot side dishes. This appetizer is a combination of two tartares, totally different in character: the herring is strong and salty, while the salmon has a fine, fresh flavour. Traditional Westphalian pumpernickel is a dark, slightly sweet bread made of shredded rye grains soaked in water and then baked extremely slowly. It keeps for a long time and is one of the most typically German of all foods.

1 Wash the herring fillets under cold running water, pat dry with kitchen paper, then with a sharp knife, cut into small cubes. Place in a large bowl.

2 Stir the diced apple and onion into the herring. Add the lemon juice and chives and season with ground white pepper.

3 Cut the salmon fillet into cubes the same size as the herring and place in a separate bowl. Add the red onion and mix together, then add the oil, lemon juice and sour cream. Season with salt and ground white pepper. Stir in the dill.

4 Butter the pumpernickel slices and cut them in half diagonally. Divide the herring tartare among eight pieces and the salmon tartare among the remainder.

5 Garnish with snipped chives or a sprig of dill and serve on a board. Alternatively, arrange some salad leaves on individual plates and top with the bread slices.

Energy 255kcal/1057kJ; Protein 18.1g; Carbohydrate 4g, of which sugars 3.3g; Fat 15.9g, of which saturates 4.4g; Cholesterol 62mg; Calcium 41mg; Fibre 0.7g; Sodium 85mg

Serves 4

For the herring tartare

200g/7oz matjes herring fillet

1 small apple, peeled and finely diced

1 small onion, finely diced

juice of ½ lemon

15ml/1 tbsp snipped fresh chives

ground white pepper

For the salmon tartare

200g/7oz skinless, boneless salmon fillet

1 small red onion, finely diced

15ml/1 tbsp sunflower oil

juice of ½ lemon

20ml/4 tsp sour cream

15ml/1 tbsp chopped fresh dill

salt and ground white pepper

To serve

8–10 slices pumpernickel

butter, for spreading

snipped chives and dill sprigs, to garnish

Serves 4

600g/1lb 6oz Lyoner or other boiling sausage

150g/5oz Emmental cheese

1 white onion

5 gherkins, halved lengthways then finely sliced

15ml/1 tbsp finely chopped parsley

salt, ground white pepper and sugar

sourdough or dark rye bread and butter, to serve

For the dressing

50ml/3 tbsp sunflower oil

25ml/1½ tbsp white wine vinegar (preferably herb-flavoured)

pinch of ground paprika

Cook's tip A good way of using any leftovers for a main course is to mix the sausage salad with cooked pasta. Season it again and very quickly you have a German pasta salad.

Rhenish sausage salad with Emmental
Rheinischer Wurstsalat mit Emmentaler

Germans love sausages, so it seems logical to include a salad that has sausage as its main ingredient. The best kind to use for this is the Lyoner, a boiling sausage that is a speciality of the Saarland in south-west Germany, but you can use frankfurters instead if you can't find it. Emmental cheese originated in neighbouring Switzerland, but is also produced in Germany and is very popular there. Instead of Emmental cheese a mature Gouda gives a stronger taste, as does Tilsiter cheese, although purists would not approve.

1 Slice the sausage thinly and place in a large bowl. Cut the Emmental cheese into small cubes and add to the sausage.

2 With a sharp knife, slice the white onion into very thin slices and separate them into rings. Add the onion rings to the sausage and cheese and mix. Add the sliced gherkin to the bowl and mix again.

3 To make the dressing, blend the oil and vinegar in a small bowl or jar, whisk thoroughly to blend, then season with salt, pepper, sugar and a pinch of paprika and whisk again.

4 Pour the dressing over the sausage and cheese mixture and toss together until all the ingredients are coated in the dressing. Add the chopped parsley and leave to stand for at least 1 hour. Serve with slices of buttered sourdough or rye bread.

Energy 647kcal/2682kJ; Protein 28.1g; Carbohydrate 16.1g, of which sugars 5.5g; Fat 52.3g, of which saturates 20.4g; Cholesterol 120mg; Calcium 459mg; Fibre 2.1g; Sodium 1675mg

Potato salad with frankfurters
Pellkartoffelsalat mit Frankfurter Würstchen

Potato salad is a classic dish in every region of Germany. There are many different ways to prepare it, and this is a lighter version without mayonnaise. It tastes best when freshly made and eaten at room temperature.

1 Put the unpeeled potatoes in a pan with the caraway seeds and bay leaves. Boil in salted water until tender. Remove from the heat, drain and leave to cool. When cool enough to handle, peel and slice the potatoes and place in a bowl.

2 Heat the oil in a frying pan over medium heat and sweat the diced onion and bacon. Add the vinegar and chicken stock and season with salt, pepper and sugar. Bring to the boil, remove from the heat and stir the mixture into the potato. Add the herbs and sliced cucumber to the bowl. Set aside for the flavours to blend.

3 Put the frankfurters in a pan with cold water to cover and heat gently. Simmer for 8–10 minutes until heated through. Don't allow the water to boil or the frankfurters will burst. Serve with the potato salad and mustard.

Energy 536kcal/2234kJ; Protein 22.2g; Carbohydrate 42.5g, of which sugars 11g; Fat 31.9g, of which saturates 10.8g; Cholesterol 85mg; Calcium 66mg; Fibre 4g; Sodium 1276mg

Serves 4

750g/1¾lb waxy potatoes

5ml/1 tsp caraway seeds

3 bay leaves

15ml/1 tbsp sunflower oil

2 white onions, finely diced

100g/3½oz bacon, diced

15ml/1 tbsp white wine vinegar

250ml/8fl oz/1 cup chicken stock

small bunch fresh parsley and small bunch fresh chives, finely chopped

1 cucumber, halved lenthways, seeds removed, finely sliced

8 frankfurters

salt, ground white pepper and sugar

medium-hot mustard, to serve

Serves 4

50g/2oz/4 tbsp butter

1 onion, chopped

1 garlic clove, chopped

400g/14oz parsnips, peeled and cut into chunks

100ml/3 ½fl oz/scant ½ cup apple juice

pinch of freshly grated nutmeg

500ml/17fl oz/generous 2 cups chicken stock

100ml/3 ½fl oz/scant ½ cup single (light) cream

100ml/3 ½fl oz/scant ½ cup sour cream

15ml/1 tbsp sunflower oil

12 slices Black Forest ham, cut into fine strips

salt and ground white pepper

chopped parsley, to garnish

Parsnip soup with Black Forest ham
Pastinakensuppe

Before the potato conquered German cuisine in the 18th century, the parsnip was the most common vegetable, and its distinctive sweet flavour is still very popular. Black Forest ham is seasoned with juniper, garlic, pepper and other spices, then cured for several weeks over burning spruce wood. It has a strong, smoky flavour and is probably the most famous of all German hams.

1 Melt the butter in a large pan over medium heat. Gently fry the onions and garlic for about 3 minutes, until softened. Add the parsnips and stir in the apple juice. Season with salt, pepper and nutmeg and add the stock. Bring to the boil, turn down the heat and simmer for 20 minutes, until the parsnips are soft.

2 Blend until smooth using a hand blender or in a food processor. Stir in both the cream and sour cream and return to the boil.

3 Heat the oil in a frying pan over high heat and fry the strips of ham until they are crisp. Pour the soup into hot bowls and sprinkle with ham and chopped parsley.

Energy 304kcal/1266kJ; Protein 12g; Carbohydrate 17.8g, of which sugars 10.6g; Fat 21g, of which saturates 11.1g; Cholesterol 73mg; Calcium 77mg; Fibre 4.8g; Sodium 718mg

50g/2oz/4 tbsp butter

1 onion, roughly chopped

1 garlic clove, roughly chopped

500g/1¼lb carrots, roughly chopped

1 large apple, peeled, cored and roughly chopped

100ml/3½fl oz/scant ½ cup Riesling

500ml/17fl oz/generous 2 cups vegetable stock

100ml/3½fl oz/scant ½ cup apple juice

200ml/7fl oz/scant 1 cup single (light) cream

100ml/3½fl oz/scant ½ cup crème fraîche

15ml/1 tbsp pumpkin seeds and 5ml/ 1 tsp snipped fresh chives, to garnish

salt and ground white pepper

Carrot and apple cream soup
Karotten-Apfelcreme

Combining the sweetness of carrots with the fruity taste of apples and a creamy consistency creates a wonderful soup that you can enjoy at any time of year. Roasted pumpkin seeds add a crunch to the soup's velvety texture.

1 Melt the butter in a pan over medium heat. Add the onions and cook for 5 minutes until softened. Add the garlic and cook for a few minutes more. Stir in the carrots and the apples.

2 Add the Riesling, followed by the stock and the apple juice. Season with salt and pepper. Bring to the boil, reduce the heat and simmer for 15 minutes.

3 Add the cream and the crème fraîche and bring the soup to the boil again. Blend the soup with a hand blender. If it seems too thick, add some more stock.

4 Heat a frying pan over medium heat and dry-fry the pumpkin seeds for 3 minutes, until toasted, stirring occasionally. Sprinkle with salt. When serving the soup, sprinkle some pumpkin seeds on top and scatter with chives.

Energy 341kcal/1412kJ; Protein 3g; Carbohydrate 18.2g, of which sugars 16.5g; Fat 27.2g, of which saturates 16.8g; Cholesterol 71mg; Calcium 84mg; Fibre 3.7g; Sodium 150mg

Asparagus soup with North Sea prawns
Spargelsuppe mit Büsumer Krabben

Büsumer prawns (shrimp) are a speciality of the fishing town of Büsum in Schleswig-Holstein, but you can use Atlantic prawns instead. Traditionally this soup is made with white asparagus, but green can also be used.

1 Peel the asparagus, retaining the peelings, and cut the spears into 5mm/¼in pieces. Put the peelings in a pan with 1.5 litres/2½ pints/6¼ cups cold water, bring it to the boil, lower the heat and simmer for about 20 minutes. Strain and reserve the stock. There should be about 1 litre/1¾ pints/4 cups.

2 In another pan, melt the butter, add the flour and stir over low heat for 2 minutes to make a roux. Gradually add the wine followed by the asparagus stock, stirring constantly. Stir in the asparagus pieces, lemon juice and cream, and season with salt, pepper and nutmeg. Bring back to the boil and simmer for 5 minutes.

3 Remove the pan from the heat and stir the egg yolks into the hot soup to enrich the colour and texture. Divide the prawns among four soup plates and ladle the soup over them. Garnish with chopped parsley and serve immediately.

Energy 618kcal/2553kJ; Protein 45.3g; Carbohydrate 37.6g, of which sugars 26.9g; Fat 30.4g, of which saturates 14.8g; Cholesterol 213mg; Calcium 440mg; Fibre 21.6g; Sodium 196mg

Serves 4

500g/1¼lb white or green asparagus

50g/2oz/4 tbsp butter

50g/2oz/½ cup plain (all-purpose) flour

100ml/3½fl oz/scant ½ cup Riesling

juice of 1 lemon

200ml/7fl oz/scant 1 cup single (light) cream

pinch of freshly grated nutmeg

2 egg yolks, lightly beaten

115g/4oz peeled North Sea prawns (shrimp)

salt and ground white pepper

15ml/1 tbsp chopped parsley, to garnish

Cook's tip Asparagus stock can sometimes be bitter. To avoid this, add a bread roll to the pan while cooking the stock to absorb any bitterness.

Potato soup with sausages
Kartoffelsuppe mit gebratenen Würstchen

Served with slices of fried frankfurter sausage, this dish is a real German classic. Try to use floury potatoes, because they produce a smoother texture when they are blended. Marjoram is the perfect herb for this soup: if you can't get it fresh, add a little dried marjoram when cooking the vegetables.

1 Melt the butter in a large pan over medium heat. Gently fry the onions and garlic for about 3 minutes, until softened. Add the potatoes, leek and carrot to the pan and pour in the stock. Bring to the boil and season with salt, pepper and nutmeg. Simmer for about 15 minutes, until the potatoes are soft.

2 Blend the soup until smooth using a hand blender or in a food processor. Stir in both the single cream and the sour cream and return to the boil.

3 Heat a frying pan over high heat. Add some oil and fry the slices of sausage for 1–2 minutes until the edges are crisp. To serve the soup, pour it into hot bowls, scatter some sausage slices on top and sprinkle with chopped marjoram.

Energy 597kcal/2477kJ; Protein 12.5g; Carbohydrate 57.8g, of which sugars 43.7g; Fat 36.5g, of which saturates 18.1g; Cholesterol 93mg; Calcium 195mg; Fibre 13.8g; Sodium 690mg

Serves 4

50g/2oz/4 tbsp butter

1 onion, roughly chopped

1 garlic clove, chopped

2 medium potatoes, peeled and roughly chopped

½ leek, roughly chopped

1 medium carrot, roughly chopped

500ml/17fl oz/generous 2 cups chicken stock

pinch of freshly grated nutmeg

100ml/3½fl oz/scant ½ cup single (light) cream

100ml/3½fl oz/scant ½ cup sour cream

15ml/1 tbsp sunflower oil

salt and ground white pepper

4 frankfurter sausages, thinly sliced, and fresh marjoram, chopped, to garnish

Serves 4

50g/2oz/4 tbsp butter

1 onion, chopped

1 leek, sliced

400g/14oz can sauerkraut

1 medium potato, peeled and diced

pinch of caraway seeds

2 bay leaves

100ml/3½fl oz/scant ½ cup apple juice

500ml/17fl oz/2 generous cups
chicken stock

200ml/7fl oz/scant 1 cup single
(light) cream

100ml/3½fl oz/scant ½ cup sour cream

200g/7oz bacon, finely diced

salt and ground white pepper

chopped parsley, to garnish

Sauerkraut soup with bacon
Sauerkrautsuppe mit krossem Speck

There are many ways to prepare sauerkraut – why not try it in a soup? It's important to strike the right balance between the sourness of the sauerkraut, the sweetness of the apple juice and the strong, salty flavour of the bacon. The cream adds smoothness and the caraway adds an extra dimension.

1 Melt the butter in a large pan over medium heat. Gently fry the chopped onion and leek for about 3 minutes, until softened.

2 Add the sauerkraut, diced potato, caraway seeds and bay leaves, and season well. Add the apple juice and stock and bring to the boil. Reduce the heat and simmer gently for about 30 minutes, then blend until smooth using a hand blender or in a food processor. Stir in both the cream and sour cream and return to the boil.

3 Heat a frying pan over high heat and fry the bacon until it is crisp and browned. Pour the soup into hot bowls, scatter some bacon on top and sprinkle with chopped parsley.

Energy 437kcal/1814kJ; Protein 13.7g; Carbohydrate 21.3g, of which sugars 9.5g; Fat 33.5g, of which saturates 19.1g; Cholesterol 98mg; Calcium 145mg; Fibre 4.3g; Sodium 1499mg

SNACKS & LIGHT MEALS

Bavarian platter

Perfect spring vegetables with crayfish

Spätzle with cheese and onions

Potato pancakes with smoked salmon

Scrambled eggs with prawns and smoked eel

Nuremberg sausages with apple sauerkraut

Apple and potato mash with black pudding

A selection of German food favourites

Small, tasty dishes are included in this chapter, several of them regional favourites using ingredients such as North Sea prawns (shrimp), Bavarian ham and cheese, or local sausage. These recipes are especially suitable for a snack during the day, or maybe a light lunch or supper. However, the size of the portions can easily be doubled, so most of them also work well as a main course. The Bavarian recipe for Brotzeit is a perfect example. This is an open sandwich topped with ham, gherkins and cheese, a typical snack from the south of Germany. Its perfect accompaniment is a glass of strong, cloudy Weissbier, an unusual and refreshing drink made with wheat and yeast. Germans would eat this kind of Brotzeit as a snack in the afternoon or as a cold supper in the evening.

One real German speciality is spätzle, a kind of pasta. This originated in the south of the country, but is now popular everywhere in Germany. The difference between Italian pasta and spätzle is that these fresh noodles are first boiled in water and then gently pan-fried in butter or baked in the oven.

Good cheese is another staple food for a snack. France may be the first country that comes to mind as the place to buy the best cheese, but German dairy farmers make many excellent quality cheeses, and also a wide variety of different kinds. There are cheeses available made from cow's, goat's or sheep's milk, in all strengths from mild and light to rich and dark. They all have their particular qualities, and make a great snack, served simply with buttered bread.

Bavarian platter
Bayrische Brotzeit

Brotzeit (literally 'bread time') is a Bavarian expression, and this meal includes some specialities of the region, such as obazta, a mixture of ripe Camembert, butter and onion. Serve on large wooden boards.

1 To make the obatza, mash the Camembert with a fork and stir in the onion, butter and cream cheese. Season the mixture to taste with paprika, caraway, salt and pepper, stir in the beer and turn into a small bowl. To make the salad, grate the radish into a bowl. Whisk together the oil and vinegar, season to taste and pour the dressing over the radish. Toss thoroughly.

2 Put the sausages in a pan with water to cover and heat gently to simmering point. Cook for about 8 minutes, without boiling. Serve in a bowl of hot water if you wish to keep the sausages warm.

3 Arrange the ham and cheese slices on a wooden board and garnish with gherkins and parsley. Butter the bread and sprinkle with chopped chives. Serve with the bowls of radish salad and obazta, with some sweet mustard on the side.

Energy 664kcal/2757kJ; Protein 29g; Carbohydrate 20.7g, of which sugars 4.4g; Fat 52g, of which saturates 28.6g; Cholesterol 145mg; Calcium 546mg; Fibre 2.5g; Sodium 1598mg

Serves 4

4 Bavarian veal sausages

8 slices smoked ham

8 slices Emmental or Limburger cheese

4 slices sourdough bread

butter, for spreading

15ml/1 tbsp snipped chives

gherkins and parsley, to garnish

sweet mustard, to serve

For the obazta

200g/7oz Camembert

1 small onion, finely chopped

50g/2oz/4 tbsp butter, softened

50g/2oz/¼ cup cream cheese

pinch each paprika and ground caraway seed

15ml/1 tbsp beer, preferably wheat beer

salt and ground white pepper

For the radish salad

400g/1¼lb white radish, peeled

15ml/1 tbsp sunflower oil

10ml/2 tsp cider vinegar

salt, ground white pepper and sugar

200g/7oz cauliflower, divided into small florets

200g/7oz young carrots, peeled and sliced

50g/2oz/4 tbsp butter

200g/7oz white asparagus, peeled and cut into pieces

100ml/3½fl oz/scant ½ cup apple juice

100g/3½oz fresh morels

100ml/3½fl oz/scant ½ cup single (light) cream

pinch of freshly grated nutmeg

100g/3½oz sugar snap peas

150g/5oz cooked crayfish tails

salt and ground white pepper

chopped parsley, to garnish

Perfect spring vegetables with crayfish
Leipziger Allerlei

This can be eaten as a side dish, but actually it is so good that it deserves to be served on its own. The recipe is from Saxony in the heart of Germany, and when you see it on a menu it is a sure sign that spring has begun. Asparagus, sugar snap peas, young carrots and morels – all represent the new season. If you can't get crayfish, use prawns.

1 Blanch the cauliflower florets and carrots for 4–5 minutes in boiling water. Drain and refresh under cold running water. The vegetables should still be crisp.

2 Melt the butter in a large pan. Add the asparagus and toss briefly over high heat, so that the stems are shiny. Add the apple juice to the pan and bring to a simmer. Add the cauliflower and carrot and the morels. Cook for 4–5 minutes.

3 Stir in the cream and season with salt, pepper and nutmeg. Add the sugar snap peas and crayfish tails and cook until heated through, then transfer to a serving dish and serve immediately, garnished with parsley.

Energy 235kcal/974kJ; Protein 11.2g; Carbohydrate 11.1g, of which sugars 10.3g; Fat 16.4g, of which saturates 10g; Cholesterol 82mg; Calcium 88mg; Fibre 3.8g; Sodium 182mg

Spätzle with cheese and onions
Kässpätzle

Spätzle is the German form of pasta from Swabia, a region of southern Germany. It's important to get the consistency of the dough right and to beat some air into it: you'll see bubbles coming up when it's ready. Traditionally, the dough is smoothed out thinly on a wooden board using the hands and then chopped into thin strips with a knife, but it's easier to use a potato ricer.

1 Preheat the oven to 200°C/400°F/Gas 6. Put the flour in a bowl and make a well in the centre. Add the eggs, water, oil and nutmeg, and beat to make a firm dough. Continue beating for 2–3 minutes until bubbles start to rise.

2 Bring a large pan of salted water to the boil. Put the dough into a potato ricer and, holding it over the pan, push carefully until strips of dough start to emerge and fall into the water. When the spätzle float to the surface they are done. Remove them with a slotted spoon and transfer to a bowl of cold water, then drain.

3 Butter a baking tray and spread a layer of spätzle over the base. Cover with a layer of grated cheese, then repeat, ending with a layer of cheese. Bake for 7–10 minutes until the cheese is melted and lightly browned.

4 Meanwhile, heat the oil in a pan over high heat and fry the onions, stirring occasionally, until browned. Scatter them over the baked spätzle.

5 Put the lettuce in a salad bowl. Mix the yogurt with the lemon juice and chives and season to taste with salt, pepper and sugar. Pour the dressing over the lettuce, garnish with the tomatoes and serve with the spätzle.

Energy 900kcal/3778kJ; Protein 41.4g; Carbohydrate 111.5g, of which sugars 13.3g; Fat 34.8g, of which saturates 16.6g; Cholesterol 350mg; Calcium 818mg; Fibre 6.3g; Sodium 832mg

Serves 4

500g/1¼lb plain (all-purpose) flour

6 eggs, lightly beaten

250ml/8fl oz/1 cup lukewarm water

5ml/1 tsp sunflower oil

pinch of freshly grated nutmeg

25g/1oz/2 tbsp butter

250g/9oz/2¼ cups grated Emmental cheese

15ml/1 tbsp sunflower oil

2 onions, thinly sliced

salt and ground white pepper

For the salad

1 lettuce

150ml/¼ pint/⅔ cup natural (plain) yogurt

juice of ½ lemon

15ml/1 tbsp snipped chives

pinch of sugar

100g/3½oz cherry tomatoes, halved, to garnish

salt and ground white pepper

Cook's tip Cook the strands of dough in small batches so as not to overcrowd the pan, and bring the water back to a fast boil for each batch.

Potato pancakes with smoked salmon
Reibekuchen mit Lachs aus dem Rauch

Potato pancakes are very easy to make and can be served in many different ways, both savoury and sweet. Here, they are partnered with smoked salmon and a cool sour cream dressing with fresh herbs, but you can use any other smoked fish you prefer, or try them for breakfast with fried eggs.

1 To make the pancakes, mix the potatoes, onions, flour and eggs together and season with nutmeg, salt and pepper. Heat some oil in a frying pan over high heat.

2 Drop spoonfuls of the mixture into the pan to form small pancakes, about 6cm/2½in in diameter and 1cm/½in thick, and fry for 2–3 minutes on each side. Remove and drain on kitchen paper while you cook the rest of the pancakes.

3 Mix the sour cream with the lemon juice and the chopped herbs, and season with salt, pepper and a pinch of sugar.

4 Arrange the pancakes on a serving plate with the smoked salmon and garnish with salad leaves. Spoon some dressing over and serve the rest separately.

Energy 711kcal/2982kJ; Protein 37.5g; Carbohydrate 76.9g, of which sugars 16g; Fat 30.4g, of which saturates 11.1g; Cholesterol 224mg; Calcium 185mg; Fibre 6.6g; Sodium 1773mg

Serves 4

For the pancakes

1.5kg/3lb potatoes, peeled and finely grated

3 onions, finely chopped

10ml/2 tsp plain (all-purpose) flour

3 eggs

pinch of freshly grated nutmeg

sunflower oil, for frying

salt and ground white pepper

For the sour cream dressing

250ml/8fl oz/1 cup sour cream

juice of ½ lemon

handful each of fresh parsley, chives and dill, finely chopped

pinch of sugar

salt and ground white pepper

To serve

12 slices smoked salmon

salad leaves, to garnish

Scrambled eggs with prawns and smoked eel
Rührei mit Nordseekrabben und Räucheraal

Fishermen swear by this dish because it's so nutritious, and they prepare it on board ship. North Sea prawns are very special and have more flavour than those from the Atlantic. Fished from the Wadden Sea off the German coast, the prawns are cooked and peeled immediately on the fishing boats, ready for sale when they land. If you can't find them use Atlantic prawns.

1 Beat the eggs and season with salt and pepper. Stir in the chives.

2 Melt the butter in a frying pan over medium heat. Pour in the eggs and cook them, stirring constantly, for 3–4 minutes, until they are just set. Remove from the heat and stir in the prawns.

3 Quickly butter the slices of bread or toast and top each piece with scrambled egg and a few pieces of smoked eel. Serve immediately.

Energy 477kcal/1987kJ; Protein 32.4g; Carbohydrate 14.4g, of which sugars 0.7g; Fat 33g, of which saturates 14.8g; Cholesterol 596mg; Calcium 141mg; Fibre 1.6g; Sodium 603mg

Serves 4

8 eggs

15ml/1 tbsp snipped chives

50g/2oz/4 tbsp butter, plus extra for spreading

300g/11oz peeled North Sea or Atlantic prawns (shrimp)

200g/7oz smoked eel fillets, cut into pieces

4 thick slices sourdough bread or toast

salt and ground white pepper

Nuremberg sausages with apple sauerkraut
Nürnberger Rostbratwürste auf Apfelsauerkraut

These little sausages are among Germany's finest. Only as long as your finger, they should weigh no more than 25–30g/1oz apiece. Restaurants offer them in portions of a dozen or half dozen, and they make a perfect snack with sauerkraut and beer. *Guten Appetit und Prost*!

1 Heat the butter in a large pan over medium heat and gently fry the bacon and onion for about 3 minutes. Add the sauerkraut, the spices and the apple juice. Cook for 30 minutes, stirring occasionally and adding more apple juice if needed. Add the apple cubes and grated carrots and cook for a further 5 minutes.

2 Blend the potato flour to a smooth paste with a little apple juice or water and stir it into the sauerkraut. As it comes back to the boil, the remaining juices will thicken and the sauerkraut will become shiny. Season to taste with salt, pepper and sugar, then spoon into a serving dish and keep warm.

3 Heat the oil in a frying pan over high heat, and fry the sausages for 6–10 minutes, turning frequently, until they are browned on all sides and cooked through. Arrange the sausages on top of the sauerkraut and garnish with chopped parsley. Serve with mustard and sourdough bread.

Energy 644kcal/2675kJ; Protein 18.6g; Carbohydrate 34g, of which sugars 17.5g; Fat 49.1g, of which saturates 19.8g; Cholesterol 81mg; Calcium 159mg; Fibre 5.2g; Sodium 2207mg

Serves 4

25g/1oz butter

50g/2oz bacon, diced

1 onion, chopped

500g/1¼lb canned sauerkraut

3 allspice berries

3 bay leaves

2.5ml/½ tsp caraway seeds

200ml/7fl oz/scant 1 cup apple juice

1 apple, peeled, cored and diced

2 carrots, grated

5ml/1 tsp potato flour (potato starch)

30ml/2 tbsp oil

24 Nuremberg sausages

salt, ground white pepper and sugar

chopped parsley, to garnish

medium-hot mustard and sourdough bread, to serve

Serves 4

45ml/3 tbsp oil

2 onions, chopped

500g/1¼lb apples, peeled and diced

juice of 1 lemon

5ml/1 tsp sugar

100g/3½oz/7 tbsp butter

500g/1¼lb floury potatoes, boiled

100g/3½oz bacon

500g/1¼lb black pudding (blood sausage)

pinch of freshly grated nutmeg

salt and ground white pepper

15ml/1 tbsp chopped parsley, to garnish

Variation If you don't like black pudding, replace it with mini burgers made from minced (ground) pork, or some sliced spicy sausages.

Apple and potato mash with black pudding
Himmel und Erde mit Gebratener Blutwurst

In German this dish is known as 'heaven and earth'– heaven for the apple, and earth for the potato. The recipe comes from Westphalia in the middle of Germany, and is a winning combination of fruity and savoury ingredients.

1 Heat 15ml/1 tbsp oil in a pan over medium heat and cook the onions for 2–3 minutes. Add the apple, lemon juice, sugar and 15ml/1 tbsp water. Simmer gently until the apple is soft, and add the butter. Add the apple mixture to the hot boiled potatoes and mash together. Season with salt, pepper and nutmeg. Keep warm.

2 Heat the remaining oil in two frying pans over high heat. Fry the bacon cubes in one for 4–5 minutes until crisp and browned. Slice the black pudding and fry the slices in the other pan until browned on both sides.

3 Spoon the mash on to four plates, then put the fried black pudding on top and sprinkle some bacon cubes over it. Garnish with chopped parsley.

Energy 855kcal/3559kJ; Protein 20.8g; Carbohydrate 61g, of which sugars 19.7g; Fat 60.4g, of which saturates 26.7g; Cholesterol 156mg; Calcium 193mg; Fibre 4.9g; Sodium 1767mg

FISH DISHES

Fried trout, miller's wife-style

Matjes herring with bacon and onions

Fried catfish with cucumber salad

Fish fillets in creamy mustard sauce

Rhenish mussels with root vegetables

Nutritious and delicious

Germany has good access to the sea around the northern coast and plenty of lakes and rivers all over the country, so there are many German recipes for fish and shellfish. White and oily fish such as cod, plaice, herring or mackerel from the sea, or pike, perch, trout and catfish from freshwater lakes are all very popular.

Fish contains valuable nutritional elements, such as protein and iodine, and is generally low in calories. What is more, it is easy to prepare, and quick to cook. In this chapter, different ways of preparing fish are described, for example frying, simmering in a sauce or baking. Most of these recipes are suitable for whole fish or fillets.

One real favourite in Germany and, indeed, in most countries around the North Sea and Baltic coasts, is matjes. This popular way of conserving herring comes originally from Holland (hence the Dutch name) and it is very popular as a snack, particularly in the northern part of the country near the coast. The herring are salted and marinated in vinegar and spices. When the matjes season starts in June, fish lovers make a special pilgrimage to Bremen, where the first cask of fresh herring is opened with great ceremony.

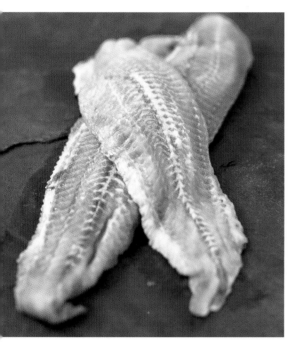 

Fried trout, miller's wife-style
Forelle Müllerin Art

In Germany this classic method of frying fish in flour is named after the miller's wife. When mills were built on, and powered by, rivers, trout and flour were both close at hand for the miller's wife to quickly produce a meal.

1 Preheat the oven to 180°C/350°F/Gas 4. Clean the fish and season inside and out with lemon juice, salt and pepper. Spread the flour on a plate and turn the fish in it to coat. Heat the oil in a large frying pan and fry the fish carefully for 3 minutes on each side until the skin is crisp. Remove the fish to a baking tray and cook in the oven for 15–20 minutes. If you can tear out the dorsal fin easily the fish is cooked. Remove the fish to a serving dish and keep warm.

2 While the fish is cooking, peel and boil the potatoes in salted water. Mix the yogurt with the lemon juice and chopped dill and season with salt, pepper and sugar. Pour it over the lettuce and tomatoes and toss together.

3 Melt the butter in a small pan. Drain the potatoes and add them to the serving dish. Pour the butter over the fish and garnish with chopped parsley and chives and lemon slices. Serve immediately, with the salad.

Energy 699kcal/2935kJ; Protein 55.1g; Carbohydrate 52.7g, of which sugars 10g; Fat 31.3g, of which saturates 16.3g; Cholesterol 250mg; Calcium 221mg; Fibre 3.9g; Sodium 438mg

Serves 4

4 fresh trout, weighing about 300g/11oz each

1 lemon, plus extra slices to garnish

30ml/2 tbsp plain (all-purpose) flour

30ml/2 tbsp sunflower oil

1kg/2¼lb potatoes

100g/3½oz butter

salt and ground white pepper

parsley and chives, chopped,   ɔarnish

For the salad

200ml/7fl oz/1 cup natural (p

juice of ½ lemon

1 lettuce, separated into leaves

2 tomatoes, sliced

salt, ground white pepper and sugar

chopped fresh dill

Serves 4

1kg/2¼lb potatoes, peeled

1kg/2¼lb green beans, trimmed

100g/3½oz butter

200g/7oz bacon, diced

3 onions, 2 chopped and 1 sliced into fine rings

8 matjes herring fillets

15ml/1 tbsp chopped fresh savory

salt and ground white pepper

Cook's tips If you can't find savory, use some fresh thyme instead.

Sauce remoulade, or tartare sauce, makes a good accompaniment for this dish.

Matjes herring with bacon and onions
Matjesfilet mit Speckstippe

Formerly a fish for the poor man's table, nowadays matjes herring is a delicacy. It is young fish, caught in the Atlantic during May and June, and is very tender, with pink flesh and a silvery skin. If you find the salty taste too strong, soak the fillets in milk for a couple of hours before cooking for a milder flavour.

1 Boil the potatoes in salted water until tender. Meanwhile, cook the trimmed beans in boiling salted water for 6–8 minutes, then drain and refresh under cold running water. They should still be crisp with a fresh green colour.

2 Heat the butter in a pan over medium heat and fry the bacon in it for about 3 minutes, then add the chopped onion. Cook for a further minute, then add the cooked beans. Season with salt and pepper and stir in the chopped savory.

3 Drain the potatoes and arrange on a serving plate with the herring fillets and the beans. Garnish with onion rings.

Energy 970kcal/4032kJ; Protein 47.4g; Carbohydrate 58.1g, of which sugars 16g; Fat 53.4g, of which saturates 26.1g; Cholesterol 203mg; Calcium 199mg; Fibre 9.8g; Sodium 1103mg

Serves 4

200g/7oz/1¾ cups plain (all-purpose) flour

200ml/7fl oz/scant 1 cup milk

3 eggs

800g/1¾lb catfish fillet

juice of 1 lemon

salt and ground white pepper

oil, for deep frying

For the salad

2 large cucumbers, cut in half lengthways and thinly sliced

250ml/8fl oz/1 cup sour cream

juice of 1 lemon

15ml/1 tbsp chopped fresh dill

pinch of sugar

salt and ground white pepper

fresh dill and lemon slices, to garnish

Cook's tip If you can't get catfish you can use another white-fleshed fish such as cod, pike or haddock instead.

Fried catfish with cucumber salad
Gebackener Waller mit Rahmgurkensalat

This is a great dish for a balmy summer night, combining a cold, creamy salad with hot fish in a crisp batter. The dish is fresh and light, but totally satisfying. It goes very well with boiled potatoes.

1 Reserving 25g/1oz/¼ cup of the flour, put the rest in a bowl and season with salt and pepper. Add the milk and eggs and beat together until you have a smooth batter. Set aside to rest.

2 To make the salad, salt the sliced cucumber and leave it to stand for 20 minutes to draw out the water. Drain in a sieve (strainer), then place in a serving bowl. Mix the sour cream with the lemon juice and dill and season to taste with salt, pepper and sugar. Add the dressing to the cucumber and fold in to mix.

3 Cut the fish into approximately 100g/3½oz chunks and season them with lemon juice, salt and pepper. Put the reserved flour on a flat plate and turn the fish pieces in it to coat them.

4 Heat the oil in a deep fryer to 190°C/375°F. Dip the fish fillets in the batter and put them straight into the hot oil. Deep-fry the fish, a few pieces at a time, for 3–4 minutes until the batter is brown and crisp. Put them on a tray and keep them warm in a low oven while you fry the rest.

5 Arrange the cucumber salad in the middle of a serving plate and put the fried fish around it. Garnish with dill and lemon slices.

Energy 725kcal/3026kJ; Protein 48.6g; Carbohydrate 44.8g, of which sugars 6.6g; Fat 40.3g, of which saturates 12.1g; Cholesterol 275mg; Calcium 268mg; Fibre 2.1g; Sodium 300mg

Serves 4

300ml/½ pint/1¼ cups fish stock
100ml/3½oz/scant ½ cup single (light) cream
10ml/2 tsp grainy mustard
1kg/2¼lb boiled potatoes, thinly sliced
150g/5oz bacon, diced into cubes
1 onion, finely chopped
small bunch chives, chopped
800g/1¾lb fish fillets (cod, salmon, trout, pike or perch)
juice of 1 lemon
oil, for frying
salt and ground white pepper
fresh dill, to garnish

Cook's tip If the sauce seems too thin, thicken it with about 5ml/1 tsp cornflour (cornstarch) slaked in a little cold water.

Fish fillets in creamy mustard sauce
Hamburger Pannfisch mit Senfsauce

This dish from northern Germany is one of my all-time favourite meals. You can use any kind of fish that is good for pan-frying, or a mix of different kinds. The mustard sauce is made with grainy mustard to add texture to the dish. Fried potatoes with bacon and onions are a perfect accompaniment.

1 Heat the fish stock and season it, if necessary, with salt and pepper. Add the cream and mustard and simmer for 5 minutes to make the sauce.

2 Heat some oil in a frying pan over high heat and fry the potato slices and the bacon until browned and crisp. Add the onion and fry for another 5 minutes. Season with salt and pepper and stir in the chives.

3 Meanwhile, season the fish with lemon juice, salt and pepper. Heat some oil in another pan and fry the fillets, turning once, until golden on both sides. Arrange the fried potatoes in the middle of a serving plate with the fish round them and pour the sauce around. Garnish with fresh dill.

Energy 570kcal/2387kJ; Protein 47.9g; Carbohydrate 42.5g, of which sugars 5.1g; Fat 24.1g, of which saturates 6.9g; Cholesterol 126mg; Calcium 62mg; Fibre 2.7g; Sodium 738mg

Rhenish mussels with root vegetables
Rheinische Muscheln mit Wurzelgemüse

Mussels are at their plumpest and best in the cooler months of the year – from September to April. In this simple dish the delicious juices from the mussels combine with the Riesling to make a wonderful sauce.

1 Peel all the vegetables. Cut the carrot and celery into fine matchsticks or dice, and thinly slice the onion. Peel and finely chop the garlic.

2 Heat the oil in a large pan over high heat. Add the mussels, the prepared vegetables and the garlic. Stir well and add the white wine and the herbs. Season with salt and pepper.

3 Cover the pan tightly and leave the mussels to cook for about 5 minutes, until the shells have opened. Discard any mussels that remain closed. Spoon into bowls and sprinkle with chopped parsley. Serve with fresh white bread.

Energy 278kcal/1169kJ; Protein 28g; Carbohydrate 16.8g, of which sugars 14.5g; Fat 6.4g, of which saturates 0.9g; Cholesterol 60mg; Calcium 376mg; Fibre 4.1g; Sodium 371mg

Serves 4

4 medium carrots

2 large sticks celery

2 medium onions

2 garlic cloves

15ml/1 tbsp sunflower oil

2kg/4½lb mussels, cleaned

300ml/½ pint/1¼ cups Riesling

2 sprigs parsley

2 sprigs thyme

2 bay leaves

salt and ground white pepper

chopped parsley, to garnish

white bread, to serve

Cook's tip Do not cook any mussels that have broken shells, or are open and do not close when sharply tapped.

MEAT DISHES

Beef with beetroot, potatoes and herring

Simmered beef topside with horseradish

Swabian beef stew with spätzle

Beef with raisin sauce and potato dumplings

Calves' liver Berlin-style

Veal meatballs in white caper sauce

Braised lamb with potatoes

Cabbage stuffed with pork

Pears, beans and bacon

Pork in aspic with remoulade sauce

Pork with cabbage and bread dumplings

Hearty and sustaining

Germany is famous for its meat dishes. Roasted in the oven, braised in stock, simmered on the hob or quickly pan-fried – there are many ways to cook meat in a traditional German style. No matter how it is cooked, there is one important element that these dishes have in common: they are served with plenty of sauce or gravy, and are often accompanied by the ubiquitous sauerkraut. Sauerkraut can be served with fried sausages, roasted pork or even in a creamy version with fried fish. Rich pork dishes, such as the classic Bavarian Schweinshaxe, go particularly well with the astringent sauerkraut and just need an accompaniment of buttered potatoes or dumplings to balance the dish.

Beef is also a popular meat in Germany, and many recipes call for long, slow cooking to make sure that the meat is really tender. Alternatively, it can be minced (ground) or chopped and served with vegetables and potatoes or dumplings.

Favourite accompaniments to meat dishes are root vegetables, which are available over the whole year, easy to store, quick to prepare and very healthy as well. Carrots, beetroots (beet), parsnips, leeks, onions and swede (rutabaga) have wonderful tastes and colours and give German meat dishes a depth of flavour and an element of sweetness.

Beef with beetroot, potatoes and herring
Labskaus

In the days before electricity and refrigerators, preserved food was vital, and this classic of north German cuisine unites pickled vegetables, cured meat and marinated fish. Labskaus brings this unexpected combination of ingredients together – traditionally, the beetroot is mashed and mixed into the meat – and it has an interesting history and a unique taste.

1 Put the beef in a pan, cover with cold water and bring quickly to the boil, skimming off the scum. Add the bay leaves and some salt and turn down the heat. Simmer for about 1½ hours until the meat is tender. Drain, reserving the stock and the beef. Put the beef in a food processor and chop it finely.

2 Mash the potatoes and stir in the herring. Heat the lard in a large pan and fry the sliced onion gently. Add the chopped beef, the potato and fish mash and 200ml/7fl oz/scant 1 cup of the reserved stock. Season with salt and pepper and mix.

3 Heat a little oil in a frying pan and fry the eggs. Divide the mash among four serving plates, top each with an egg and garnish with beetroot and gherkins.

Energy 842kcal/3504kJ; Protein 46g; Carbohydrate 32.1g, of which sugars 6.8g; Fat 57.7g, of which saturates 18.9g; Cholesterol 315mg; Calcium 82mg; Fibre 3.1g; Sodium 1111mg

Serves 4

600g/1lb 6oz salt beef brisket
3 bay leaves
675g/1½lb potatoes, peeled and boiled
2 matjes herring fillets, cut into small pieces
100g/3½oz lard
2 onions, finely sliced
4 eggs
oil, for frying
200g/7oz bottled baby beetroot (beets), cut into small pieces
300g/11oz gherkins, sliced
salt and ground white pepper
chopped parsley, to garnish

serves 4

1kg/2¼lb beef topside

2 medium carrots, roughly chopped

100g/3½oz celeriac, roughly chopped

½ leek, trimmed, cleaned and roughly chopped

2 onions, halved

3 bay leaves

4 allspice berries

5 black peppercorns

a few parsley stalks

1 parsnip, sliced

4 medium carrots, sliced

2–3 sticks celery, sliced

1 large potatoes, peeled and sliced

200g/7oz swede (rutabaga), peeled and sliced

beef stock cube (optional)

30ml/2 tbsp butter

30ml/2 tbsp plain (all-purpose) flour

45ml/3 tbsp creamed horseradish

juice of 1 lemon

200ml/7fl oz/scant 1 cup single (light) cream

30ml/2 tbsp chopped parsley

salt

Simmered beef topside with horseradish
Gesottener Tafelspitz mit Meerrettichsauce

This dish originally came from Austria but has been very popular in Germany for a long time. Slowly simmering the meat provides a delicious stock, which you then use to cook the accompanying vegetables.

1 Put the beef in a pan with cold water to cover, bring to the boil and skim off any scum. Reduce the heat and leave the meat to simmer for about 45 minutes. Add the chopped vegetables, spices and parsley stalks to the pan and continue to cook for about 90 minutes, until the beef is tender. Lift out the beef and keep it warm. Season the stock with salt to taste and reserve.

2 Put the sliced vegetables in a pan with 1 litre/1¾ pints/4 cups of the beef stock, bring to the boil, lower the heat and simmer until the vegetables are tender. Season with salt and, if the stock is not rich enough, part or all of a beef stock cube.

3 Melt the butter in a pan over medium heat and stir in the flour. Gradually add 500ml/17fl oz/generous 2 cups of the beef stock, stirring. Bring it to the boil and add the creamed horseradish, lemon juice and cream.

4 Stir the chopped parsley into the vegetables and stock, and spoon on to serving plates. Slice the beef and arrange it on top. Serve the sauce separately.

Energy 653kcal/2747kJ; Protein 65g; Carbohydrate 44.3g, of which sugars 26g; Fat 25.3g, of which saturates 13g; Cholesterol 171mg; Calcium 281.5mg; Fibre 10.8g; Sodium 576mg

Swabian beef stew with spätzle
Gaisburger Marsch

This traditional recipe comes from southern Germany and is named after a neighbourhood of Stuttgart, the biggest city in Baden-Württemberg. The heart of every stew is the stock, so make sure yours has a strong flavour. If you don't have time to make your own, buy fresh, ready-made stock.

1 Put the oxtail bones in a large pan and cover with cold water. Bring to the boil and skim off any scum. Simmer for 45 minutes, then add the mixed vegetables, the spices and the parsley stems (keep the leaves to garnish the soup). Simmer for 2–3 hours, until the meat is falling off the bones.

2 Meanwhile, prepare the spätzle. Put the flour in a bowl and make a well in the centre. Add the other ingredients and beat together to make a firm dough. Continue beating for 2–3 minutes until bubbles start to rise.

3 Bring a large pan of salted water to the boil. Put the dough into a potato ricer and, holding it over the pan, push carefully until strips of dough start to emerge and fall into the water. When the spätzle float to the surface they are done. Remove them with a slotted spoon and transfer to a bowl of cold water, then drain.

4 Strain the stock and season to taste with salt (if it is still not strong enough, add a beef stock cube). There should be about 1.5 litres/2½ pints/6¼ cups stock. Pull the meat off the bones, cut it into bitesize cubes and return it to the stock.

5 Add all the prepared vegetables to the stock, bring it back to the boil and leave it to simmer for about 10 minutes, or until they are tender. Stir in the spätzle and cook for 1–2 minutes. Serve the stew in bowls, garnished with parsley.

Serves 4

2kg/4½lb oxtail bones

500g/1¼lb mixed soup vegetables (celeriac, carrots and leeks), roughly chopped

4 bay leaves

5 allspice berries

1 bunch parsley

2 medium potatoes, diced

4 medium carrots, diced

100g/3½oz swede (rutabaga), diced

1 leek, sliced

1 large stick celery, sliced

salt

For the spätzle

165g/5½oz plain (all-purpose) flour

2 eggs

90ml/6 tbsp lukewarm water

2.5ml/½ tsp sunflower oil

pinch of freshly grated nutmeg

salt and ground white pepper

Cook's tip Add a few onion skins when making stock, to give it a wonderful golden colour.

Energy 781kcal/3285kJ; Protein 68.5g; Carbohydrate 62.7g, of which sugars 18.8g; Fat 30.4g, of which saturates 1.2g; Cholesterol 95mg; Calcium 180mg; Fibre 8.5g; Sodium 464mg

300ml/½ pint/1¼ cups red wine vinegar

300ml/½ pint/1¼ cups red wine

3 bay leaves

3 allspice berries

2 cloves

6 peppercorns

4 medium carrots, diced

2–3 sticks celery, sliced

2 onions, chopped

1kg/2¼lb beef chuck or brisket

30ml/2 tbsp sunflower oil

100g/3½oz/⅓ cup tomato purée (paste)

25g/1oz/¼ cup raisins

15ml/1 tbsp butter

15ml/1 tbsp plain (all-purpose) flour

200g/7oz each carrots, celery and
swede (rutabaga), cut into chunks

30ml/2 tbsp chopped parsley

50g/2oz butter

salt, ground white pepper and sugar

For the dumplings

1kg/2¼lb floury potatoes

2 egg yolks

150g/5oz plain (all-purpose) flour

2 slices white bread, cut into cubes

oil, for frying

salt, ground white pepper and nutmeg

Beef with raisin sauce and potato dumplings
Sauerbraten in Rosinensauce mit Klößen

This uniquely German dish comes from the Rhineland but is known all over the country. The meat must be marinated for two days to allow the delicious mixture of very sour and sweet flavours to infuse.

1 Put the vinegar in a pan with the red wine and add the spices. Bring to the boil, then add the carrots, celery and onions and cook for another 5 minutes. Remove from the heat and leave to cool. Put the beef in a non-metallic container, add the marinade and leave in the refrigerator for 2–3 days. Turn the meat every 12 hours.

2 Lift out the meat, strain the marinade, and reserve the vegetables. Season the meat with salt and pepper. Heat the oil in a large pan over high heat and seal the meat for 3 minutes on each side. Take out the meat and add the vegetables to the pan. Fry for 4 minutes, until browned. Add the tomato purée. Fry, stirring, until it darkens. Before it burns add 1.5 litres/2½ pints/6¼ cups of the marinade. Return the beef to the pan, cover and simmer over low heat for about 2 hours, skimming as necessary. Add the raisins and cook gently for another 30 minutes.

3 To make the potato dumplings, peel, boil and mash the potatoes with the egg yolks. Beat in the flour and season with salt, pepper and nutmeg.

4 Heat some oil in a frying pan over a medium heat and fry the cubes of bread for 3–4 minutes, until crisp on all sides. Drain on to paper towels. Season with salt. Form the potato into 8–10 dumplings, putting croûtons in the centre of each.

5 When the meat is nearly done, bring a large pan of salted water to the boil and drop the dumplings into the boiling water. Make sure that they do not stick to the bottom of the pan. When they rise to the top, reduce the heat and leave them to simmer for 5 minutes.

6 Take out the meat and keep it warm. Strain the sauce and return it to the pan. Season to taste. Knead the butter with the flour to make a beurre manié and stir a little at a time into the boiling sauce until it thickens. Cook for another 5 minutes.

7 Meanwhile, blanch all the remaining vegetables in boiling water for 6–7 minutes. Drain and refresh under cold running water: they should still be crisp. Heat the butter in a pan over medium heat and add the vegetables. Season with salt, pepper and nutmeg and cook, stirring, for 5 minutes. Stir in the chopped parsley. Slice the beef and serve with the dumplings and vegetables. Pour some of the sauce over the meat and serve the rest separately.

Energy 1159kcal/4857kJ; Protein 71.1g; Carbohydrate 106.6g, of which sugars 28.8g; Fat 47.1g, of which saturates 20.3g; Cholesterol 283mg; Calcium 203mg; Fibre 10g; Sodium 506mg

Serves 4

3 onions, finely sliced and separated into rings

plain (all-purpose) flour, to dust

45ml/3 tbsp sunflower oil

800g/1¾lb calves' liver, sliced 1cm/½in thick

pinch of freshly grated nutmeg

50g/2oz clarified butter

3 small apples, peeled, cored and sliced 1cm/½in thick

100ml/3½fl oz/scant ½ cup apple juice

salt and ground white pepper

chopped parsley, to garnish

mashed potato, to serve

Calves' liver Berlin-style
Kalbsleber Berliner Art

A true Berlin dish, this is very traditional and evokes memories of the city's golden period in the 1920s. The tender liver is served with crisp fried onion, glazed apples and mashed potatoes: a great mixture of tastes and textures.

1 Dust the onion rings with flour. Heat the oil in a pan over high heat and fry the onion rings for 1–2 minutes until crisp. Lift them out and drain on kitchen paper. Keep warm in a low oven.

2 Season the liver with salt, pepper and ground nutmeg and dust with flour. Heat the clarified butter in a frying pan over medium heat and fry the slices of liver for 2–3 minutes on each side. Remove from the pan and keep warm.

3 Fry the apple slices in the same pan for 2 minutes on each side. Add the apple juice and let it bubble for a few minutes to reduce, glazing the apples.

4 Arrange the liver on a serving dish with the apple slices on top, and garnish the dish with the crispy onion rings and chopped parsley. Serve with mashed potato.

Energy 584kcal/2438kJ; Protein 43.1g; Carbohydrate 29.6g, of which sugars 17.9g; Fat 33.6g, of which saturates 12.2g; Cholesterol 769mg; Calcium 71mg; Fibre 3.6g; Sodium 287mg

Veal meatballs in white caper sauce
Königsberger Klopse mit Kapernsauce

This dish comes from Königsberg, a medieval Baltic port. The mild, creamy sauce complements the veal very well. I think the capers give it a special character but if you don't like them, they can be omitted.

1 Soak the bread rolls in water, then squeeze them out, break into small pieces and place in a mixing bowl. Add the veal, onions and anchovies. Chop half the capers and add them to the bowl, with 5ml/1 tsp of the parsley and the mustard. Season, then add the eggs and mix thoroughly. Form into 12–14 meatballs.

2 Bring a pan of salted water to the boil over high heat and add the meatballs. Reduce the heat and leave to simmer for 8–10 minutes. Remove the meatballs with a slotted spoon, reserving the stock, and keep them warm in a low oven.

3 Transfer 500ml/17fl oz/generous 2 cups of the stock to a pan and bring it to the boil. Stir in the cream. Knead the butter with the flour to make a beurre manié and stir the mixture, a little at a time, into the boiling sauce until it is thickened. Add the remaining capers and let the sauce cook for 3 minutes, then put the meatballs back into it. Garnish with chopped parsley and serve with rice.

Serves 4

2 day-old white bread rolls, about 100g/3½oz total weight

1kg/2¼lb minced (ground) veal

2 onions, finely chopped

2 anchovies, finely chopped

10ml/2 tsp capers

15ml/1 tbsp chopped parsley

5ml/1 tsp medium-hot mustard

2 eggs

200ml/7fl oz/scant 1 cup single (light) cream

50g/2oz/4 tbsp butter

50g/2oz/½ cup plain (all-purpose) flour

salt and ground white pepper

boiled rice, to serve

Energy 722kcal/3018kJ; Protein 59.9g; Carbohydrate 30.1g, of which sugars 7.2g; Fat 41.2g, of which saturates 20.9g; Cholesterol 306mg; Calcium 160mg; Fibre 2g; Sodium 554mg

Serves 4

1kg/2¼lb boned leg of lamb

60ml/4 tbsp oil

2 medium carrots, cut into chunks

100g/3½oz celeriac, cut into chunks

1 onion, cut into chunks

100g/3 ½oz/⅓ cup tomato purée (paste)

300ml/½ pint/1¼ cups red wine

2 garlic cloves, halved

5 thyme sprigs

800g/1¾lb small potatoes, scrubbed, and halved

115g/4oz/8 tbsp butter mixed with 50g/2oz/½ cup plain (all-purpose) flour to make a beurre manié

2 onions, finely chopped

500g/1¼lb green beans, trimmed, boiled in salted water, then refreshed under cold running water

10ml/2 tsp chopped savory

salt and ground white pepper

Variation If you prefer, you can replace the savory with a couple of sprigs of fresh thyme.

Braised lamb with potatoes
Geschmorte Lammkeule mit Kleinen Kartoffeln

It is an old custom in Germany to eat lamb on Easter Day as a symbol of the Resurrection of Jesus. Easter is traditionally a time when families get together, and the highlight of the festival is this celebratory meal.

1 Season the lamb with salt and pepper. Heat 15ml/1 tbsp of the oil in a large flameproof casserole over high heat and brown the lamb on all sides, then remove. Add the vegetables to the pot and cook for 4 minutes until browned.

2 Add the tomato purée. Stir occasionally and allow the paste to darken. Before it starts to burn, pour in the red wine and about 2 litres/3½ pints/8 cups water. Bring to the boil and skim, then add the garlic and thyme and reduce the heat. Return the lamb to the pot and leave to simmer for 2–2½ hours.

3 After the lamb has been cooking for about an hour, preheat the oven to 160°C/325°F/Gas 3. Put the potatoes in a roasting tin (pan). Season and toss in the remaining oil. Put them in the oven and cook for 35–40 minutes, increasing the temperature to 200°C/400°F/Gas 6 for the last 10 minutes to crisp them.

4 When the lamb is done, lift it out and keep it warm. Strain the sauce and discard the vegetables. Bring the sauce to the boil again and stir in the beurre manié, a little at a time, to thicken it to the right consistency. Season to taste.

5 Heat the remaining butter in a pan over medium heat and add the onion. Fry gently for 2–3 minutes, then add the cooked beans and the chopped savory. Add salt to taste and cook, stirring, for 2 minutes. Carve the lamb into slices and serve with the sauce, accompanied by the beans and potatoes.

Energy 1113kcal/4641kJ; Protein 59.7g; Carbohydrate 65.4g, of which sugars 22.7g; Fat 64.4g, of which saturates 30.1g; Cholesterol 256mg; Calcium 179mg; Fibre 9.7g; Sodium 553mg

Cabbage stuffed with pork
Kohlrouladen mit Speckstreifen

This dish reminds me of my mother. I really loved her cooking, especially her Kohlrouladen. This way of stuffing cabbage leaves is popular all over Germany, though the spices used vary slightly from region to region.

1 Soak the bread rolls in water, then squeeze them out and break into small pieces. Put the pieces into a large mixing bowl. Add the pork, eggs and mustard and season with salt, pepper, caraway and paprika. Use your hands to mix well.

2 Trim the base from the cabbage leaves. Blanch in boiling salted water for 6 minutes, then drain and refresh under cold running water. Dry thoroughly. Place a spoonful of the meat filling in the lower centre of each cabbage leaf. Flip the sides of the leaf over the filling and roll it up. Secure the end with a cocktail stick (toothpick).

3 Preheat the oven to 160°C/325°F/Gas 3. Heat a little oil in a frying pan over high heat and fry the cabbage rolls for 2 minutes on each side. As they are done, take them out and place them in a baking dish. Add the onion and bacon to the pan and fry for 2 minutes, then add the stock. Bring to the boil and pour the contents of the pan over the cabbage rolls. Bake for about 15 minutes. Garnish with chopped parsley and serve with mashed potatoes.

Energy 683kcal/2847kJ; Protein 54g; Carbohydrate 23.2g, of which sugars 8.7g; Fat 42.4g, of which saturates 12.4g; Cholesterol 254mg; Calcium 110mg; Fibre 2.8g; Sodium 1074mg

Serves 4

2 day-old white bread rolls, about 100g/3½oz total weight

800g/1¾lb minced (ground) pork

2 eggs

5ml/1 tsp medium-hot mustard

pinch of ground caraway seeds

pinch of paprika

8 large leaves from a white cabbage

oil for frying

2 onions, chopped

200g/7oz smoked bacon, diced

200ml/7fl oz/scant 1 cup chicken stock

salt and ground white pepper

chopped parsley, to garnish

mashed potatoes, to serve

Serves 4

15ml/1 tbsp oil

4 pieces smoked bacon about 1cm/½in thick, 400g/14oz total weight

700g/1½lb green beans, trimmed

4 small pears, peeled, quartered and cored

500g/1¼lb potatoes, peeled and cut into 1cm/½in cubes

5ml/1 tsp chopped fresh savory

15ml/1 tbsp plain (all-purpose) flour

4 slices of bacon

Variation If no savory is available, use the leaves from a couple of sprigs of fresh thyme.

Pears, beans and bacon
Birnen, Bohnen und Speck

This is a good example of a classic north German dish where people like to eat food that combines sweet, sour, salty and smoky flavours. Very popular all over the region, it is simple, hearty, warming food at its best.

1 Heat the oil in a pan over medium heat and fry the bacon pieces for 2–3 minutes on each side. Add 1 litre/1½ pints/4 cups water to the boil, then reduce the heat, cover and simmer for 15–20 minutes. Add the trimmed beans, pears, potatoes and chopped savory and cook, covered, for a further 20–30 minutes.

2 Take out the bacon, pears and vegetables using a slotted spoon and keep them warm. Mix the flour with some water and stir it into the remaining liquid in the pan. Bring it to the boil, stirring, until it thickens. Return the bacon, pears and vegetables to the pan and season. Fry the bacon slices, then serve each piece of bacon with some beans, potatoes, pears and some sauce, topped with a fried slice of bacon.

Energy 438kcal/1829kJ; Protein 23.2g; Carbohydrate 41.9g, of which sugars 18.8g; Fat 20.8g, of which saturates 6.8g; Cholesterol 53mg; Calcium 104mg; Fibre 8.5g; Sodium 1558mg

Pork in aspic with remoulade sauce
Sauerfleisch mit Remouladensauce

This hearty, home-style German dish is popular all over the country, eaten with a glass of beer. It takes some time to prepare the pork in aspic, but this is done in advance and the rest of the meal is quickly assembled.

1 Put the pork in a large pan with the bay leaves and spices. Add water to cover, bring to the boil and skim, then reduce the heat, cover and simmer for 1 hour.

2 Peel and trim the vegetables, cut into small dice and reserve. Add the peelings and some salt to the meat pan. Continue to cook gently for 1–1½ hours, until the meat is tender. Lift it out and leave it to cool, then cut into 5mm/¼in cubes.

3 Strain the stock and measure out 700ml/1¼ pints/3 cups. Put it in a pan, bring it to the boil and add the vinegar and the diced vegetables. Cook for 5 minutes, then remove from the heat. Soak the gelatine leaves in cold water for 5 minutes, squeeze out the excess water and add them to the hot stock. Stir until the gelatine has dissolved, and season to taste with salt and sugar.

4 Line a 900g/2lb loaf tin (pan) with enough clear film (plastic wrap) to hang over the edges. Pack in the meat and the diced vegetables, then top up with stock. Chill for at least 4 hours until the jelly is set, removing it from the refrigerator 20 minutes before serving to come to room temperature.

5 Put all the ingredients for the remoulade sauce in a food processor or blender, and blend on high power for 1 minute. Season to taste. Turn out the pork and remove the clear film. Cut into 1cm/½in thick slices. Garnish with parsley and tomato slices and serve with the remoulade sauce.

Energy 530kcal/2197kJ; Protein 29.8g; Carbohydrate 6.5g, of which sugars 5.5g; Fat 42.9g, of which saturates 7.3g; Cholesterol 113mg; Calcium 56mg; Fibre 2g; Sodium 331mg

Serves 4

600g/1lb 6oz boneless pork shoulder

3 bay leaves

5 peppercorns

1 clove

2 each of allspice and juniper berries

2 medium carrots

2–3 sticks celery

1 onion

150ml/¼ pint/⅔ cup white wine vinegar

15 gelatine leaves

salt and sugar

chopped parsley and sliced tomatoes, to garnish

For the remoulade sauce

250ml/8fl oz/1 cup mayonnaise

75g/3oz gherkins and 20ml/4 tsp vinegar from the jar

1 onion, roughly chopped

5ml/1 tsp capers

10ml/2 tsp chopped parsley

5ml/1 tsp chopped dill

salt and sugar

Cook's tip Pan-fried potatoes make a very good accompaniment to this dish.

Serves 4

4 pork knuckles with bones and skin, about 700g/1½lb each

30ml/2 tbsp oil

2 onions, roughly chopped

2 garlic cloves, halved

500ml/17fl oz/ 2 cups dark beer

3 bay leaves

5ml/1 tsp caraway seeds

salt and ground white pepper

For the bread dumplings

45ml/3 tbsp oil

6 day-old white bread rolls (about 350g/12oz total weight), broken into pieces

1 small onion, finely chopped

50g/2oz smoked bacon, finely diced

250ml/8fl oz/1 cup milk

pinch of freshly grated nutmeg

10ml/2 tsp chopped parsley, plus extra to garnish

5ml/1 tsp snipped chives

2 egg yolks

For the cabbage

15ml/1 tbsp oil

100g/3½oz smoked bacon, diced

1 small onion, finely chopped

700ml/1¼ pints/3 cups chicken stock

10ml/2 tsp white wine vinegar

1 kg/2¼lb white cabbage, quartered, cored and finely sliced

5ml/1 tsp caraway seeds

salt, ground white pepper and sugar

Pork with cabbage and bread dumplings
Schweinshaxe mit Bayrisch Kraut und Semmelknödeln

Pork knuckle is synonymous with German eating culture. Whether cured, cooked and served cold, or roasted to give it a crispy skin, this economical cut is aromatic, flavoursome and tender, but it needs long, slow cooking.

1 Preheat the oven to 180°C/350°F/Gas 4. Heat the oil in a large flameproof casserole over a high heat. Season the pork and fry, turning, for 6 minutes. Add the onion and garlic and fry for another 2 minutes. Deglaze the pan with the beer, then add 1 litre/1¾ pints/4 cups water, bay leaves and caraway seeds. Bring to the boil, cover and cook in the oven for 2½–3 hours, turning the knuckles occasionally.

2 Meanwhile, make the bread dumplings. Heat 30ml/2 tbsp oil in a frying pan over medium heat and fry the bread for 3–4 minutes, until crisp. Remove from the pan and put them in a large bowl. Heat the remaining oil in the pan and fry the onions and bacon for 2 minutes. Add the milk, nutmeg, salt and pepper. Bring to the boil, then pour the milk over the fried bread cubes. Add the chopped herbs and the egg yolks and mix. Leave for 20 minutes for the bread to absorb the liquid.

3 To prepare the cabbage, heat the oil in a pan over high heat and fry the bacon and onions for 2–3 minutes. Add the stock, vinegar and cabbage. Season with salt, pepper and sugar and add the caraway seeds. Reduce the heat, cover, and leave to cook for 30 minutes, stirring occasionally, until the cabbage is soft.

4 While the cabbage is cooking, form the bread mixture into eight dumplings. Bring a pan of salted water to the boil, add the bread dumplings and simmer for 20–25 minutes. When the meat is ready, arrange some of the cabbage on each plate together with a pork knuckle and some of the juices from the pot. Put two bread dumplings on each plate and garnish with a little chopped parsley.

Energy 1377kcal/5743kJ; Protein 89.1g; Carbohydrate 70.1g, of which sugars 26.6g; Fat 81.2g, of which saturates 23.1g; Cholesterol 420mg; Calcium 392mg; Fibre 8.4g; Sodium 1365mg

POULTRY & GAME DISHES

Chicken fricassée

Chicken in Riesling with roast potatoes

Roast duck with cabbage and potatoes

Roast goose with chestnut stuffing

Duck legs with red cabbage

Venison goulash with potato cakes

Wild boar with sprouts and poached pears

Farmed and wild favourites

The deep forests of the German countryside are home to many different wild birds, as well as small and large game. These are not cooked as everyday dishes – it is a special occasion when game is on the menu. There is still a strict season for game and although you can buy foreign and deep-frozen game, many people prefer fresh, locally caught meat. The hunting season for large game such as deer and wild boar is from May to January, while the season for wild birds runs from November until February.

Chicken and turkey are very popular meats nowadays, because of the reasonable price and their constant availability in the shops. German cooks are using them more and more for everyday dishes, both roasted whole and in the form of pieces simmered in a rich sauce.

Autumn and winter are the prime seasons for eating duck and goose, but they would not be cooked for everyday meals in Germany; they are mostly served on special occasions such as Christmas Day or St Martin's Day in November. The roasted bird is the highlight of the meal, presented whole at the table and then carved. The roast meat is usually accompanied by dumplings, red cabbage and a strong gravy, to make a mouthwatering dish suitable for a big family dinner.

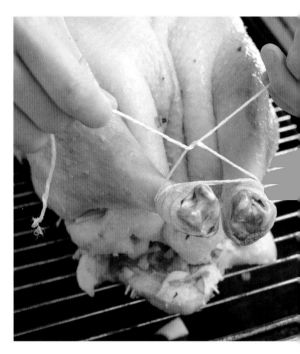

Serves 4

1 chicken (approximately 1.5kg/3½lb)

2 bay leaves

3 allspice berries

30ml/2 tbsp oil

200g/7oz mushrooms, quartered

2 small onions, sliced

400g/14oz white asparagus, peeled and cut into small pieces

200g/7oz frozen peas

200ml/7fl oz/1 cup single (light) cream

juice of 1 lemon

25g/1oz/2 tbsp butter, mixed with 25g/1oz/¼ cup flour to make a beurre manié

oil, for frying

salt, ground white pepper and sugar

chopped parsley, to garnish

steamed or boiled rice, to serve

Chicken fricassée
Hühnerfricassé

This creamy mix of tender chicken and fresh vegetables shows the influence of French cuisine on German food. Served with rice it is irresistible, and is a popular meal all over the country. Try different herbs such as lemon thyme, chives or chervil; you can also substitute different seasonal vegetables.

1 Put the chicken in a large pot and cover with water. Bring to the boil and skim. Add the spices and a pinch of salt and simmer for 60–90 minutes, until the chicken is tender. Lift out the chicken and leave to cool. Strain and reserve the stock. When the chicken is cold, pick the meat off the bones and cut it into bitesize pieces.

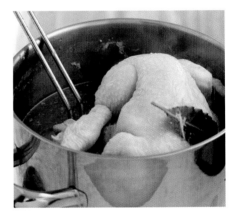

2 Heat the oil in a large pan and fry the mushrooms for 2–3 minutes over medium heat. Add the onions, asparagus and peas and fry gently for 2 minutes until softened. Pour in 500ml/17fl oz/generous 2 cups of the reserved stock and bring it to the boil. Stir in the cream and lemon juice and season to taste with salt, pepper and sugar. Whisk knobs of the beurre manié into the bubbling sauce to thicken it.

3 Finally, return the chicken to the sauce and cook gently until heated through. Garnish with chopped parsley and serve with rice.

Energy 926kcal/3832kJ; Protein 55.1g; Carbohydrate 16g, of which sugars 6.1g; Fat 71.5g, of which saturates 22.6g; Cholesterol 282mg; Calcium 118mg; Fibre 5g; Sodium 264mg

Chicken in Riesling with roast potatoes
Hühnchen in Riesling mit Kleinen Röstkartoffeln

A variation of the classic French dish, coq au vin, this German version tastes quite different because the chicken is cooked in a German white wine, not red as in the original French recipe.

1 Preheat the oven to 180°C/350°F/Gas 4. Heat 15ml/1 tbsp of the oil in a large flameproof casserole over high heat. Season the chicken joints generously and fry them on all sides until the skin is golden brown and crisp. Add the white wine, bring to the boil and transfer the dish to the preheated oven. Cook for 30 minutes.

2 Meanwhile, put the potatoes in a baking tray, season with salt and pepper and toss in the remaining oil. Put the tray in the oven and roast for 30–40 minutes.

3 Take the chicken out of the oven, remove the joints and keep them warm. Over a medium heat, cook the onions, garlic and mushrooms in juices from the chicken and the reduced wine, then add the cream and bring back to the boil. Season well.

4 Arrange one chicken leg or one breast on warmed plates. Pour over some sauce and mushrooms and garnish with chopped parsley. Serve with the roast potatoes.

Energy 1416kcal/5881kJ; Protein 63.4g; Carbohydrate 49.9g, of which sugars 20.2g; Fat 103.9g, of which saturates 52.1g; Cholesterol 414mg; Calcium 386mg; Fibre 2.6g; Sodium 414mg

Serves 4

45ml/3 tbsp oil

4 chicken legs

4 chicken breasts

250ml/8fl oz/1 cup Riesling or other dry German white wine

800g/1¾lb small potatoes, scrubbed and halved

2 onions, thinly sliced

1 garlic clove, finely chopped

200g/7oz brown cap (cremini) mushrooms

1.5l/2⅗ pints/6¼ single (light) cream

salt and ground white pepper

chopped parsley, to garnish

Variation This dish is just as delicious served with fresh noodles rather than roast potatoes.

Roast duck with cabbage and potatoes
Gebratene Ente mit Wirsingkohl und Kartoffeln

This is probably the most popular Christmas dish in Germany. Whether it's served this way or with red cabbage and dumplings, roast duck is almost compulsory for the main meal on 25 December.

1 Preheat the oven to 160°/325°F/Gas 3. Season the ducks generously inside and out. Chop the apples and two of the onions and mix them with the mugwort.

2 Stuff the ducks with the apple mixture and tie their legs with string to keep the stuffing in place. Put them in a roasting tin (pan) and roast for 1½–2 hours, until the juices run clear, basting and pouring a little water over them from time to time.

3 When the ducks are nearly done, quarter and core the cabbage and slice it thinly. Thinly slice the remaining onions. Melt the butter in a pan over medium heat and cook the onions for 2–3 minutes until transparent, then add the cabbage and the stock. Season with salt and a pinch of nutmeg and simmer for 8–10 minutes. Add the cream and bring to the boil again.

4 When the ducks are cooked, cut off the legs and breasts. Scoop out the stuffing and keep it warm with the meat. Skim off the fat from the juices in the tin, then pour into a pan and bubble up over high heat, adding some chicken stock if there is not enough liquid. Mix the flour with a little water and stir it into the boiling sauce to thicken it. Cook for another 2–3 minutes.

5 Place a duck breast and leg on each serving plate with some of the cabbage and stuffing. Pour the sauce over, garnish with parsley and serve with boiled potatoes.

Energy 996kcal/4129kJ; Protein 40.1g; Carbohydrate 29.3g, of which sugars 25.3g; Fat 80.6g, of which saturates 29.5g; Cholesterol 169mg; Calcium 183mg; Fibre 6.6g; Sodium 347mg

Serves 4

- 2 ducks (each weighing approximately 1kg/2¼lb)
- 4 apples, peeled and cored
- 5 onions
- 1 tbsp dried mugwort (see Variation box, below)
- 1 Savoy cabbage
- 50g/2oz/4 tbsp butter
- 200ml/7fl oz/scant 1 cup chicken stock, plus extra if needed
- 200ml/7fl oz/scant 1 cup single (light) cream
- 5ml/1 tsp flour
- freshly grated nutmeg
- salt and ground white pepper
- chopped parsley, to garnish
- boiled potatoes, to serve

Variation Mugwort is an aromatic herb that is thought to help with digestive problems. In the past it was smoked by the poor as a cheap substitute for tobacco. If you can't find it, use the same amount of dried sage.

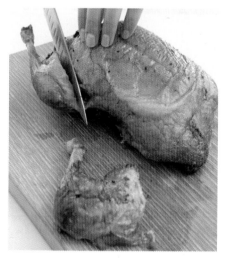

Serves 4

1 goose (approximately 3.5kg/7½lb)

15ml/1 tbsp cranberry sauce

5ml/1 tsp plain (all-purpose) flour

red cabbage to serve (see recipe on page 88)

For the stuffing

3 apples, peeled, cored and chopped

2 onions, chopped

500g/1¼lb chestnuts, cooked, peeled and chopped

salt and ground white pepper

Cook's tip As it cooks, a goose releases a lot of excess fat. Don't throw this away, as it will keep in the refrigerator, and can be used for making the best-ever roast potatoes.

Variation To make the chestnut stuffing even more rich and delicious, heat a little of the sauce in a pan and stir in 10ml/2 tsp hazelnut spread, then pour it over the stuffing.

Roast goose with chestnut stuffing
Gebratene Gans mit Kastanienfüllung

On the eve of St Martin's Day, 11 November, children walk with lanterns through the streets, singing traditional songs. On the day itself, especially in the south of Germany, many people mark the saint's day by eating roast goose. Red cabbage is the perfect accompaniment, and you could also serve some potato dumplings to complete the meal.

1 Preheat the oven to 160°C/325°F/Gas 3. Season the goose generously inside and out. Mix the chopped apples with the onions and chestnuts and stuff the goose with the mixture. Tie its legs together with string to keep the stuffing in place.

2 Put the goose in a roasting tin (pan) and roast for about 2½ hours, or until the juices run clear when the bird is pierced between the leg and the breast. Pour a little water over it from time to time. You may need to pour off the excess fat into suitable heatproof containers as the goose cooks.

3 When the goose is cooked and the juices run clear, take out of the oven and remove the legs and breasts. Scoop out the stuffing and keep it warm with the meal. Skim off the fat from the juices in the tin, then pour the juices into a pan and bubble them up over high heat, adding some chicken stock if there is not enough liquid. Stir in the cranberry sauce. Mix the flour with a little water and stir it into the boiling sauce to thicken it. Cook for another 2–3 minutes.

4 Arrange half a breast and half a leg on each serving plate, together with some of the chestnut stuffing. Pour the sauce over and serve with the red cabbage.

Energy 1159kcal/4822kJ; Protein 44.6g; Carbohydrate 56.4g, of which sugars 17.5g; Fat 85.5g, of which saturates 24.4g; Cholesterol 200mg; Calcium 91mg; Fibre 6.5g; Sodium 169mg

Duck legs with red cabbage
Knusprige Entenkeule mit Rotkohl

This is another Christmas dish, traditionally served with potato dumplings. Germans will usually use goose legs rather than duck legs, but if goose is not available, duck legs have the same rich texture and flavour.

1 To make the cabbage, chop two of the onions, melt the lard in a large pan and fry the onion for 2 minutes. Add the cabbage, vinegar, sugar, spices and apple juice, bring to the boil, cover and simmer for 30 minutes. Stir in the apples and redcurrant jelly and cook for a further 45 minutes, adding more apple juice if necessary. Towards the end of the cooking time, blend the cornflour with water and stir into the cabbage. Preheat the oven to 200°C/400°F/Gas 6.

2 While the cabbage is cooking, place the duck legs in a roasting tin (pan), season, add a cup of water and roast in the oven for 20 minutes, then reduce the temperature to 160°C/325°F/Gas 3 and cook for a further 40 minutes, basting from time to time. When the legs are cooked, lift them out and keep them warm. Add the remaining onion, chopped, and the tomato purée to the pan and fry over high heat for 3–4 minutes. Deglaze the pan with the wine and cook for another 2 minutes. Serve the duck legs with the sauce poured over, garnished with parsley and accompanied by the red cabbage. Serve with potato dumplings.

Energy 958kcal/3961kJ; Protein 20.7g; Carbohydrate 32.7g, of which sugars 28.5g; Fat 79.8g, of which saturates 22.8g; Cholesterol 12mg; Calcium 122mg; Fibre 5.1g; Sodium 146mg

Serves 4

8 duck legs or 4 goose legs

15ml/1 tbsp oil

10ml/2 tsp tomato purée (paste)

200l/7fl oz/scant 1 cup red wine

salt and ground white pepper

chopped parsley, to garnish

potato dumplings, to serve (see recipe on page 67)

For the red cabbage

3 onions

60g/2½oz lard

1 red cabbage, quartered, cored and finely sliced

100ml/3½fl oz/scant ½ cup red wine vinegar

15ml/1 tbsp sugar

2 bay leaves

3 pieces star anise

1 cinnamon stick

200ml/7fl oz/scant 1 cup apple juice

2 apples, chopped

30ml/2 tbsp redcurrant jelly

5ml/1 tsp cornflour (cornstarch)

Venison goulash with potato cakes
Hirschgoulasch mit Kartoffelplätzchen

The dark red meat and strong smell and taste of venison is very distinctive. Germany is heavily forested, so venison, wild boar and hare are on the menu throughout the country. This rich goulash is served with potato cakes.

1 Rub the meat with the spices and some oil and leave overnight. Next day, heat 3–4 tbsp oil in a large pan over high heat and fry the venison for 5–6 minutes on each side. Add the chopped onion and cook for another 4–5 minutes.

2 Add the tomato purée, red wine and the stock to the pan and bring to the boil. Reduce the heat and simmer for 40 minutes or until the meat is tender, adding more stock if necessary. Add the mushrooms and cook for a further 20 minutes.

3 Meanwhile, boil the potatoes in salted water until tender, then drain and mash. Beat in the egg yolks, flour, butter and chives and season with salt and nutmeg. When cool enough to handle, form into 8–10 cakes. Heat a little oil in a large frying pan over medium heat and fry the cakes for 2–3 minutes on each side.

4 Just before serving, stir the sour cream and gin into the venison goulash. Serve immediately with the hot, golden brown potato cakes.

Energy 618kcal/2591kJ; Protein 4g; Carbohydrate 8g, of which sugars 7.1g; Fat 20g, of which saturates 5.7g; Cholesterol 4mg; Calcium 30.5mg; Fibre 1.5g; Sodium 36.5mg

Serves 4

800g/1¾lb boneless venison, cubed

3 bay leaves

5 juniper berries, crushed

1 cinnamon stick

2 onions, chopped

10ml/2 tsp tomato purée (paste)

300ml/½ pint/1¼ cups red wine

1 litre/2¾ pints/4 cups chicken stock

250g/9oz brown cap (cremini) mushrooms, quartered

15ml/1 tbsp sour cream

200ml/7fl oz/scant 1 cup gin

oil, for frying

salt and ground white pepper

For the potato cakes

500g1¼lb floury potatoes, peeled

3 egg yolks

15ml/1 tbsp flour

50g/2oz/4 tbsp butter

oil for frying

salt and freshly grated nutmeg

small bunch chives, chopped

Serves 4

2 onions, chopped

2 carrots, chopped

100g/3 oz celeriac, chopped

2 garlic cloves, halved

3 bay leaves

5 allspice berries, 5 peppercorns and 5 juniper berries, crushed

1 litre/1¾ pints/4 cups buttermilk

1kg/2¼lb boneless leg of wild boar

15ml/1 tbsp oil

15ml/1 tbsp tomato purée (paste)

400ml/14fl oz/1⅔ cups red wine

500ml/17fl oz/2 cups chicken stock

10 slices smoked bacon

50g/2oz butter

salt and ground white pepper

spätzle, to serve (see recipe on page 43)

For the sprouts

500g/1¼lb Brussels sprouts

1 onion, peeled and finely chopped

50g/2oz smoked bacon, diced

115g/4oz/½ cup butter

For the poached pears

10ml/2 tsp sugar

250ml/8fl oz/1 cup white wine

1 cinnamon stick

2 pears, peeled, halved and cored

cranberry sauce

Wild boar with sprouts and poached pears
Wildscheinbraten

The taste of wild boar is pretty special but, like other game, it is apt to dry out during roasting. Marinating it for two to three days and then wrapping in bacon helps to keep the meat succulent. The sweet poached pears and buttery Brussels sprouts complement it perfectly. Serve with spätzle.

1 Mix two onions, carrots, celeriac, garlic and spices with the buttermilk in a lidded container and put the meat into it. Cover and leave in the refrigerator for two days to tenderize the meat and moderate its flavour.

2 Preheat the oven to 160°C/325°F/Gas 3. Lift the meat out of the marinade. Drain and reserve the vegetables and spices. Season the meat with salt and pepper. Heat the oil in a large frying pan over high heat and sear the meat for 5–6 minutes on each side, then remove to a roasting tin (pan).

3 Add the vegetables from the marinade to the pan and brown them, together with the tomato purée, for 5 minutes until they are on the point of burning. Then add the red wine and the stock. Stir well and bring the mixture to the boil, then pour it over the meat. Lay the bacon slices over the meat, securing them with cocktail sticks (toothpicks), and roast for 2–2½ hours.

4 To cook the pears, heat the sugar in a pan over medium heat until it melts and turns golden brown, then plunge the base of the pan into a bowl of cold water to stop the sugar burning. Add the white wine and the cinnamon, bring to the boil, then add the pears. Cover the pan, reduce the heat and simmer gently for 8–10 minutes until the pears are tender, then drain. Fill the cavities in the fruit halves with cranberry sauce. Keep warm until ready to serve.

5 Bring a pan of salted water to the boil and blanch the Brussels sprouts for 6–7 minutes, then drain them and refresh in cold water. Melt half the butter over medium heat, add the onion and diced bacon and fry gently for 2–3 minutes, then add the sprouts, season and cook for a further 2–3 minutes. Stir well.

6 When the meat is done, lift it out of the pan and keep warm. Fry the spätzle in butter over medium heat for 3–4 minutes until golden. Season and keep warm.

7 Strain the juices from the roasting pan into a pan and heat quickly until boiling, then stir in the butter. Slice the meat and serve with the sauce, accompanied by the bacon, pears, Brussels sprouts and spätzle.

Energy 848kcal/3538kJ; Protein 72.8g; Carbohydrate 29.7g, of which sugars 25.5g; Fat 37.6g, of which saturates 15.6g; Cholesterol 226mg; Calcium 131mg; Fibre 10g; Sodium 1487mg

PUDDINGS & DESSERTS

Red fruit jelly Hamburg-style

Semolina flummery with strawberries

Poor knights with apples

Apple fritters with fruits in rum

Apple strudel with vanilla sauce

Baked apples with marzipan

Bavarian cream with berries

Fruit treats and creamy delights

Germans love to eat desserts and a main meal is just not complete without something sweet to round it off. There is a wide range of delicious pudding recipes in German cuisine and the classics are brought together here. These happy endings combine the sweetness of the dessert itself with the freshness of juicy fruits of the season.

The spices used in desserts are imported from faraway countries through long-established trade routes, and it is a well-founded tradition in Germany to use exotic spices in sweet dishes of all kinds. Star anise, cinnamon, vanilla and marzipan were expensive in former times and it was the privilege of the rich to use such delicate flavourings. Times have changed and it is now very easy to buy spices in any supermarket at an affordable price, but fresh spices still add glamour and an unexpected twist to many German desserts.

Many of the fruits in these recipes are seasonal, but out of season there are plenty of alternatives to try. For example, fresh local strawberries will not be available in the autumn and winter, but plums, pears or other autumn fruits work very well instead. While in the north desserts are often served cold, in the south hot dishes are more popular, such as warm apple strudel flavoured with marzipan and topped with a vanilla pouring sauce.

Red fruit jelly Hamburg-style
Hamburger Rote Grütze

A wonderful and simple dessert. During the summer it can be made with fresh berries, but you can also use frozen fruit. Though it comes from the northern region, this well-known compote is eaten all over Germany.

1 Heat the sugar in a pan over medium heat until it caramelizes. When it turns golden brown, plunge the base of the pan in a bowl of cold water to stop the sugar burning. Stir in the grape juice, add the spices and return to the heat.

2 Mix the cornflour with a little cold water. When the juice comes to the boil, stir in the cornflour mixture and cook, stirring, for 1 minute to thicken.

3 Halve any large berries, and add them all to the hot juice, bring to the boil again, then remove from the heat and leave to cool. Spoon the cold compote into bowls, decorate with mint leaves and serve with cream.

Energy 86kcal/366kJ; Protein 1.1g; Carbohydrate 21.3g, of which sugars 17.8g; Fat 0.2g, of which saturates 0g; Cholesterol 0mg; Calcium 31mg; Fibre 1.3g; Sodium 13mg

Serves 4

20g/¾oz caster (superfine) sugar

200ml/7fl oz/scant 1 cup red grape juice

2 pieces of star anise

1 cinnamon stick

15g/½oz/2 tbsp cornflour (cornstarch)

450g/1lb mixed berries (strawberries, blueberries, cranberries, blackberries, raspberries or redcurrants), washed

fresh mint leaves, to decorate

single (light) cream, to serve

Serves 4

300ml/½ pint/1¼ cups milk

25g/1oz caster (superfine) sugar, plus extra for sprinkling

pinch of salt

5g/2.5ml vanilla sugar or 2.5ml/½ tsp vanilla extract

10ml/2 tsp butter

150ml/¼ pint/⅔ cup orange juice

40g/1½oz/¼ cup semolina

400g/14oz/3½ cups strawberries

Semolina flummery with strawberries
Griessflammerie mit Erdbeeren

You can eat this dessert warm or cold but serve it in small portions because it's filling. Puddings of this kind are very popular in Germany, and are useful when you are entertaining as they can be prepared in advance.

1 Heat three-quarters of the milk in a pan, together with the sugar, salt, vanilla sugar and butter. When the milk comes to the boil, remove from the heat and add the orange juice.

2 Mix the semolina with the remaining milk and stir it into the boiling milk in the pan. Cook over medium heat, stirring constantly, for 3 minutes, until it thickens, then pour the flummery into four bowls. If you intend to serve it cold, chill for 1–2 hours.

3 Hull the strawberries and cut the larger ones into smaller pieces. Sprinkle with sugar. Serve the flummery topped with strawberries.

Energy 153kcal/646kJ; Protein 4.6g; Carbohydrate 27.3g, of which sugars 19.6g; Fat 3.6g, of which saturates 2.1g; Cholesterol 10mg; Calcium 115mg; Fibre 1.4g; Sodium 71mg

Serves 4

2 eggs

400ml/14fl oz/1⅔ cups milk

grated rind of 1 lemon

½ tsp vanilla extract

pinch of salt

60ml/4 tbsp breadcrumbs

4 thick slices of day-old white bread

50g/2oz/4 tbsp butter

25g/1oz/2 tbsp caster (superfine) sugar mixed with 5ml/1 tsp ground cinnamon

For the apple compote

10ml/2 tsp caster sugar

200ml/7fl oz/scant 1 cup apple juice

juice of 1 lemon

4 apples, peeled, cored and diced

5ml/1 tsp raisins

Poor knights with apples
Armer Ritter mit Apfelragout

This recipe comes from Mecklenburg, West Pomerania and Brandenburg. *Armer Ritter* means 'poor knights', perhaps because it's a way of using up the previous day's bread. Children love it for breakfast as well as dessert.

1 Make the apple compote first. Heat the sugar in a pan over medium heat until it caramelizes. When it turns golden brown, plunge the base of the pan into a bowl of cold water to stop the sugar burning. Stir the apple juice and lemon juice into the caramel. Stir in the apples and raisins and cook for 6–7 minutes. Remove from the heat and leave to cool.

2 Beat the eggs lightly and mix in the milk, grated lemon rind, vanilla extract and a pinch of salt. Dip the bread slices into this mixture and then turn them in the breadcrumbs to coat them on both sides.

3 Melt the butter in a frying pan over medium heat and fry the bread slices for 2–3 minutes on each side, until golden. Sprinkle the sugar and cinnamon mix over the top and serve immediately, with the apple compote.

Energy 404kcal/1706kJ; Protein 11.3g; Carbohydrate 58.8g, of which sugars 33.5g; Fat 15.7g, of which saturates 8.7g; Cholesterol 130mg; Calcium 204mg; Fibre 2.5g; Sodium 461mg

Apple fritters with fruits in rum
Apfelkrapfen mit Rumtopf

Fruit fritters are a very popular dessert in Germany. At festivals you can smell them cooking from far off, and the aroma draws you like a magnet. Here, they are served with Rumtopf, a delicious traditional German preserve.

1 Mix the flour and milk in a bowl and add the baking powder, sugar and salt. Melt the butter in a small pan until it starts to brown, then mix it into the batter.

2 Heat the oil in a deep-fryer to 180°C/350°F. Peel and core the apples and cut them into thick rings. Dip them in the batter, making sure that they are completely covered, then drop them straight into the hot oil and deep-fry for 2–3 minutes, until the batter is crisp and golden brown.

3 Drain the fritters on kitchen paper, dust with icing sugar and serve immediately with a spoonful of fruit from the Rumtopf.

Energy 391kcal/1644kJ; Protein 5.5g; Carbohydrate 54g, of which sugars 16.8g; Fat 18.6g, of which saturates 2.8g; Cholesterol 4mg; Calcium 213mg; Fibre 2.4g; Sodium 205mg

Serves 4

200g/7oz/1¾ cups self-raising (self-rising) flour

100ml/3½fl oz/scant ½ cup milk

5ml/1 tsp baking powder

40g/1oz caster (superfine) sugar

pinch of salt

5ml/1 tsp butter

2 apples

oil, for deep-frying

icing (confectioners') sugar, to dust

Rumtopf, to serve (see page 16)

Variation If you don't have any Rumtopf, lightly poach a mixture of berries with sugar, rum and water, to make a quick version of a compote.

Apple strudel with vanilla sauce
Apfelstrudel mit Vanillesauce

Originally from Austria, this dessert is so good that it quickly migrated into Germany, and today it is an absolute classic. The difficult part is stretching the strudel dough until it is really thin: my first head chef told me that you should be able to read a newspaper through it. For the filling, choose eating apples that hold their shape well when cooked and have a tart, fruity flavour.

1 Mix the flour with the oil and water to make a smooth dough. Put it in an oiled bowl, cover and leave for 30 minutes in a warm place.

2 To make the filling, soak the raisins in the brandy for 20 minutes. In the meantime, slice the apples thinly, put them in a bowl and mix with the lemon juice. Add the vanilla sugar, sugar, chopped hazelnuts and breadcrumbs.

3 Preheat the oven to 160°C/325°F/Gas 3. Spread a clean dish towel on the work surface and dust it with flour. Roll out the dough on the towel, then stretch it carefully on all sides using your hands, until it is the same size as the cloth. It should now be very thin.

4 Spoon the apple filling along the lower part of the dough, leaving a space of 4cm/1½in on each side. Brush all the edges with melted butter. Turn in the sides of the dough, then use the towel to help you roll up the strudel around the filling. Brush with the rest of the melted butter and transfer it carefully to a baking tray lined with baking parchment.

5 Bake for 20–30 minutes, until the pastry is golden brown and crisp. Remove the strudel from the oven and leave it to cool for a few minutes.

6 While the strudel is baking, make the sauce. Cut the vanilla pod in half lengthways and scrape out the seeds. Put the milk and cream in a pan with the vanilla pod and seeds. Heat to boiling point, then remove from the heat.

7 Whisk the egg yolks with the sugar until light and thick, then whisk in the hot milk (having removed the vanilla pod). Set the bowl over a pan of simmering water and heat the sauce gently, stirring all the time, until it thickens. Make sure you do not overheat the mixture or the eggs will curdle.

8 When ready to serve, dust the strudel with icing sugar. Serve warm, cut into slices, and accompanied by the vanilla sauce.

Energy 525kcal/2207kJ; Protein 8.9g; Carbohydrate 69.6g, of which sugars 41g; Fat 24.9g, of which saturates 11.6g; Cholesterol 195mg; Calcium 151mg; Fibre 3.1g; Sodium 228mg

Serves 4

100g/3½oz strong white (bread) flour, plus extra for dusting

5ml/1 tsp sunflower oil, plus extra for brushing

30–35ml/6–7 tsp lukewarm water

50g/2oz/4 tbsp butter, melted

icing (confectioners') sugar, to dust

For the filling

10ml/2 tsp raisins

10ml/2 tsp brandy

400g/14oz apples, peeled and cored

juice of 1 lemon

5ml/1 tsp vanilla sugar (about) or 2.5ml/½ tsp vanilla extract

100g/3½oz caster (superfine) sugar

25g/1oz/¼ cup hazelnuts, finely chopped

50g/2oz/1 cup breadcrumbs

For the vanilla sauce

1 vanilla pod (bean)

200ml/7fl oz/scant 1 cup milk

100ml/3½fl oz/scant ½ cup single (light) cream

3 egg yolks

25g/1oz caster (superfine) sugar, or to taste

Baked apples with marzipan
Bratapfel mit Rosinen-Marzipanfüllung

This is a traditional recipe for the winter, when apples were once the only fresh fruits available and cooks needed to be really creative to find different ways to serve them. It's a comforting hot dessert: when you eat it you won't mind at all that the range of local fruit is so small at this time of year.

1 Preheat the oven to 160°C/325°F/Gas 3. Soak the raisins in the brandy for 20 minutes. Meanwhile, core the apples. Cut a small slice off the bottom of each one, if necessary, so that they will stand up. Score the skin around the apple in three places to prevent it rolling up during baking.

2 Mix the marzipan with the lemon juice, chopped pistachio nuts and raisins, and push the filling into the centre of the apples. Put the apples on a baking tray lined with baking parchment, and bake them for 20–25 minutes. Serve the apples warm with vanilla sauce.

Energy 150kcal/631kJ; Protein 2.2g; Carbohydrate 22.9g, of which sugars 22.7g; Fat 5.3g, of which saturates 0.6g; Cholesterol 0mg; Calcium 23mg; Fibre 2.3g; Sodium 33mg

Serves 4

5ml/1 tsp raisins

10ml/2 tsp brandy

4 large, crisp eating apples, such as Braeburn

75g/3oz marzipan, chopped

juice of ½ lemon

20g/¾oz/¼ cup chopped pistachio nuts

vanilla sauce, to serve (see page 101)

Serves 4

300ml/½ pint/1¼ cups milk

1 vanilla pod (bean)

4 egg yolks

150g/5oz/1¼ cups caster (superfine) sugar

7 gelatine leaves, soaked in water for 10 minutes

10ml/2 tsp almond liqueur

300ml/½ pint/1¼ cups double (heavy) cream, whipped until stiff

mint leaves, to decorate

compote of berries or fresh strawberries, to serve

Bavarian cream with berries
Bayrisch Creme mit Beeren

Every apprentice German chef has to learn this classic recipe. A soft, sweet cream with the unique aroma of fresh vanilla, served with a compote of cherries or strawberries, it makes a delightful end to a meal.

1 Put the milk in a pan. Cut the vanilla pod in half lengthways and scrape out the seeds. Add the pod and the seeds to the milk and heat to boiling point, then remove the pan from the heat.

2 Whisk the egg yolks with the sugar until light and thick, then whisk in the hot milk (discard the vanilla pod). Set the bowl over a pan of simmering water and heat the mixture very slowly, stirring, until it thickens. Remove the pan from the heat.

3 Take the gelatine leaves out of the water and squeeze out any excess. Place the leaves in a small pan with the liqueur and heat until melted, then stir this mixture into the custard. Fold the whipped cream into the custard.

4 Divide the mixture among four serving bowls and chill for 3 hours until set. Serve with a compote of cherries, or fresh strawberries, decorated with mint leaves.

Energy 587kcal/2443kJ; Protein 6.8g; Carbohydrate 45.8g, of which sugars 45.8g; Fat 47.1g, of which saturates 24.8g; Cholesterol 304mg; Calcium 171mg; Fibre 0g; Sodium 81mg

CAKES & BREADS

German cheesecake with raisins

Butter cake with caramelized almonds

Streusel plum cake

Black Forest gateau

Stollen

German ring cake

Frankfurt crown cake

Gingerbread

Onion bread

Sourdough rye bread

Caraway seed rolls

Sweet treats and baking delights

Some of the most famous cakes in the world come from Germany. There is a strong tradition of home baking, and in the south, in particular, many people bake their own cakes for Sunday afternoon tea at home. There are fierce contests between cooks as to who makes the best cake, and secret recipes have often been handed down within families and are jealously guarded. The best-known German cake is probably Black Forest gateau, but there are many other very delicious cakes to try. Recipes for some of the most popular ones follow, including gingerbread and stollen, two essential components of a German Christmas.

More than 600 different kinds of bread are baked in Germany – the country's bakers are truly world champions in the field, with every region making its own speciality. Wheat and rye bread are the most popular varieties, especially the dark rye bread that makes such a tasty snack. To German people, bread is really soul food, and just thinking of a slice of dark sourdough bread with butter and cheese or ham can make a travelling German long to be back home.

Bread and bread rolls are eaten at all times of day, as a vital component of breakfast and lunch, and also at dinnertime, when many families have a simple meal based on slices of bread with a variety of sausages, ham and cheese. It is not difficult to bake bread, but it does take time and patience, and that is why most of the bread eaten in Germany is bought from bakeries and supermarkets. But it is really worth baking your own bread at home – once the basic dough is made, it is so easy to add extra flavours, such as fresh herbs, onions, garlic, poppy or caraway seeds, or even cheese.

Makes 12 slices

For the base

130g/4½oz/generous ½ cup butter

65g/2½oz/⅓ cup caster (superfine) sugar

pinch of salt

1½ tsp vanilla extract or 2 packs vanilla sugar (about 10g/¼oz)

250g/9oz/2¼ cups plain (all-purpose) flour

For the filling

100g/3½oz/¾ cup raisins

25ml/5 tsp almond liqueur

100g/3½oz/scant ½ cup butter, softened

100g/3½oz/½ cup caster sugar

2 tsp vanilla extract or 2 packs vanilla sugar (about 10g/¼oz)

3 eggs, separated

pinch of salt

500g/1¼lb curd (farmer's) cheese

250ml/9fl oz/generous 1 cup sour cream

grated rind of 1 lemon

15ml/1 tbsp plain flour

icing (confectioners') sugar, for dusting

German cheesecake with raisins
Käsekuchen mit Rosinen

So German! This cake is famous all over the world, though in many places you can't get good curd cheese, so cream cheese is used instead. The cake is really easy to make and tastes fantastic. You can vary the dried fruit if you like – apricots are particularly good in this.

1 Preheat the oven to 190°C/375°F/Gas 5. Soak the raisins in the liqueur for 30 minutes. Butter a springform 30cm/12in cake tin (pan).

2 To make the base of the cake, cream the butter with the sugar, vanilla extract or sugar and salt. Add the flour and rub it in with the fingers to make a stiff dough. Cover the bowl with clear film (plastic wrap) and put it in the refrigerator.

3 To make the filling, cream the butter with the sugar and vanilla extract or sugar, then add the egg yolks and salt and beat until creamy. Fold in the curd cheese, sour cream, lemon rind, soaked raisins and flour. Beat the egg whites until stiff and forming peaks, then fold them gently into the mixture.

4 Roll out the dough for the cake base and press it into the prepared tin. It should be no thicker than 1cm/½in and should cover the base evenly.

5 Pour the filling over the base and bake the cake for about 1 hour. If the top starts to brown too much, protect it with a piece of baking parchment. When the cake is cooked, leave it to cool in the tin. Serve when cool, dusted with icing sugar.

Energy 360kcal/1506kJ; Protein 10.8g; Carbohydrate 40.2g, of which sugars 23.4g; Fat 18.7g, of which saturates 11.5g; Cholesterol 97mg; Calcium 119mg; Fibre 0.9g; Sodium 303mg

Butter cake with caramelized almonds
Butterkuchen mit Karamellisierten Mandeln

Makes about 16 pieces

250ml/8fl oz/1 cup lukewarm milk

40g/1½oz fresh yeast

50g/2oz/¼ cup caster (superfine) sugar

7.5ml/1½ tsp vanilla extract

pinch of salt

2 eggs

500g/1¼lb/5 cups plain (all-purpose) flour, plus extra for dusting

50g/2oz/4 tbsp butter, softened, plus extra for greasing

For the topping

100g/3½oz/7 tbsp butter

200g/7oz/1¾ cups flaked (sliced) almonds

50g/2oz/¼ cup caster sugar

100ml/3½fl oz/scant ½ cup single (light) cream

This cake is especially popular in the northern part of Germany. It doesn't contain any fruit and you're likely to have most of the ingredients in the store cupboard, so it is the perfect cake to make for unexpected visitors.

1 Pour the milk into a mixing bowl and whisk in the crumbled yeast, sugar, vanilla extract, salt and eggs. Gradually beat in the flour and the butter. Knead the dough for 3–4 minutes, until it leaves the sides of the bowl clean. Dust the dough with flour, cover it and put it in a warm place for 30 minutes or until doubled in volume.

2 To make the topping, melt the butter over medium heat, add the almonds and cook, stirring, until they are evenly browned. Add the sugar and cream and bring to the boil again. Remove from the heat and leave to cool. Preheat the oven to 180°C/350°F/Gas 4.

3 Butter a baking tray 40x30cm/16x12in and dust it with flour. Roll out the dough on the tray and leave it to rest for 15 minutes. Then spread the almond topping over it and bake for about 30 minutes until the surface is golden brown. Turn out and cool on a wire rack; cut into squares to serve.

Energy 306kcal/1279kJ; Protein 7.1g; Carbohydrate 32.7g, of which sugars 8.6g; Fat 17.2g, of which saturates 6.8g; Cholesterol 50mg; Calcium 107mg; Fibre 1.9g; Sodium 94mg

Streusel plum cake
Pflaumenkuchen mit Streuseln

This kind of cake, with a shortcrust base and a crumble topping, can be made with various different fruits, depending on the time of year. Plums are harvested from the end of summer until the middle of autumn, and while they are in season every German bakery sells fresh plum cake.

1 Preheat the oven to 180°C/350°F/Gas 4. Put the butter in a bowl with the sugar, salt, vanilla, eggs and flour. Rub the mixture with your fingertips until it is crumbly.

2 Use half the crumble dough to line a 40x30cm/16x12in baking tray, pressing it evenly over the base and up the sides. Put in the halved plums and sprinkle the sugar on top. Scatter the rest of the crumble on top of the plums.

3 Bake the cake in the preheated oven for 45–60 minutes. Dust with icing sugar and cut into squares to serve with whipped cream.

Energy 265kcal/1115kJ; Protein 3.5g; Carbohydrate 39.9g, of which sugars 20.9g; Fat 11.3g, of which saturates 7g; Cholesterol 53mg; Calcium 55mg; Fibre 1.5g; Sodium 105mg

Makes about 16 pieces

200g/7oz/scant 1 cup butter, softened

150g/5oz/¾ cup caster (superfine) sugar

pinch of salt

1½ tsp vanilla extract or 2 packs vanilla sugar (about 10g/¼oz)

2 eggs

400g/14oz/3½ cups plain (all-purpose) flour

icing (confectioners') sugar, to dust

For the filling

800g/1¾lb plums, halved and stoned (pitted)

100g/3½oz/½ cup caster sugar

whipped double (heavy) cream, to serve

Black Forest gateau
Schwarzwälder Kirschtorte

Famous all over the world, this is the archetypal German cake. The name explains its origin, but it is eaten everywhere in Germany. It's laden with calories, but don't think about that while you're eating it, just enjoy it!

1 Break up the chocolate and melt it in a bowl over a pan of gently simmering water. Preheat the oven to 160°C/325°F/Gas 3. Butter a 30cm/12in cake tin (pan).

2 Cream the butter with the sugar and vanilla extract or sugar. Gradually beat in the egg yolks, until the mixture is light and foamy. Mix in the melted chocolate. Beat the egg whites with a pinch of salt until stiff and fold them into the mixture. Sift the flour with the baking powder and fold in. Turn the mixture into the prepared tin and bake for 45–60 minutes, until a skewer pushed into the centre comes out clean. Leave to cool a little in the tin, then take out and leave on a rack to cool completely.

3 Strain the juice off the cherries, reserving the fruit, and put it in a pan. Bring to the boil, remove from the heat and add the gelatine leaves. Stir until the gelatine has dissolved, then leave to cool. Whip the cream with the vanilla until stiff.

4 Slice the cake into three layers. Sprinkle the bottom layer with half the Kirsch, then spread some of the cherry jelly over it and put half the cherries on top. Top with some cream. Put the second layer of cake on top, and repeat the layers of Kirsch, jelly, cherries and cream. Top with the final cake layer.

5 Spread cream around the sides of the cake, and pipe 12 whirls on the top, adding a glacé cherry to each. Sprinkle some of the flaked chocolate on top of the cake and press the rest into the sides. Chill for 4–5 hours before serving.

Makes about 12 slices

100g/3½oz plain (bittersweet) chocolate

100g/3½oz/7 tbsp butter, softened

100g/3½oz/½ cup caster (superfine) sugar

2 tsp vanilla extract or 3 packs vanilla sugar (about 20g/¾oz)

6 eggs, separated

pinch of salt

100g/3½oz plain (all-purpose) flour

50g/2oz/½ cup cornflour (cornstarch)

5ml/1 tsp baking powder

For the filling

500g/1¼lb bottled cherries

5 gelatine leaves, soaked in cold water for 5 minutes

750ml/1¼ pints/3 cups double (heavy) cream

5ml/1 tsp vanilla extract or 1 pack vanilla sugar (about 5g/2.5ml)

100ml/3½fl oz/scant ½ cup Kirsch

To decorate

12 glacé (candied) cherries

75g/3oz flaked chocolate

Energy 551kcal/2293kJ; Protein 5.7g; Carbohydrate 36.8g, of which sugars 26.2g; Fat 45.7g, of which saturates 25.5g; Cholesterol 196mg; Calcium 73mg; Fibre 0.5g; Sodium 128mg

Stollen
Stollen

This delicious cake, with its luxurious filling, is eaten in the period before Christmas. The recipe comes from Dresden, and only cakes made in this region can be given the name 'Christstollen'.

1 Soak the sultanas in the brandy for 3–4 hours. Preheat the oven to 160°C/325°F/Gas 3.

2 Heat the milk to about 50°C/120°F, add the yeast and stir until it has dissolved. Put the flour and sugar into a large bowl, make a well in the centre and pour in the milk. Draw in the dry ingredients and knead with both hands until you have a smooth dough. Leave to rest in a warm place for 1 hour.

3 Add the vanilla, salt, spices and the butter, cut into small pieces, and knead the dough again for 3–5 minutes.

4 Add the chopped almonds and the marzipan to the bowl and knead thoroughly into the dough. Then add the candied peel and the sultanas and knead again for at least 3 minutes.

5 Divide the dough into three pieces, and form each into a long shape with rounded ends. Line a baking sheet with baking parchment and lay the three stollen on it. Bake for 45–60 minutes, until risen and golden brown.

6 Melt some butter in a pan and brush it over the warm stollen, then dust them thickly with icing sugar and leave to cool.

Makes 3 cakes

500g/1¼lb/3½ cups sultanas (golden raisins)

100ml/3½fl oz/scant ½ cup brandy

500ml/17fl oz/generous 2 cups milk

75g/3oz fresh yeast

1kg/2¼lb plain (all-purpose) flour

150g/5oz/¾ cup caster (superfine) sugar

10ml/2 tsp vanilla extract or 3 packs vanilla sugar (about 20g/¾oz)

pinch of salt

pinch each ground cardamom, cinnamon and ginger

500g/1¼lb/2½ cups butter, plus extra for brushing

150g/5oz/1¼ cups chopped almonds

150g/5oz marzipan, chopped

100g/3½oz/⅔ cup candied lemon peel

100g/3½oz/⅔ cup candied orange peel

icing (confectioners') sugar, to dust

Cook's tip Stollen is usually made in a large batch to last over the winter months. It will keep well if wrapped up tightly and stored in a dry place.

Energy 3829kcal/16069kJ; Protein 55.8g; Carbohydrate 511.9g, of which sugars 256.5g; Fat 178.8g, of which saturates 95.3g; Cholesterol 393mg; Calcium 1065mg; Fibre 21.5g; Sodium 1590mg

German ring cake
Gugelhupf

The basis for this well-known cake is a yeast batter, which is baked in a distinctively shaped circular mould with a hole in the middle. It is one of Germany's best-loved cakes and is familiar all over Europe.

1 Soak the raisins in the brandy for 30 minutes. Meanwhile, heat the milk in a pan until just lukewarm.

2 Sift the flour into a large bowl and make a well in the centre. Crumble the yeast into the well, add the sugar and pour in the lukewarm milk. Stir the milk carefully with the sugar and yeast, gradually drawing in a little of the flour so that a thick batter forms. Cover the bowl and leave to rest in a warm place for 20–30 minutes.

3 Cream together the butter, sugar, vanilla and salt, and gradually add the eggs and baking powder. Add the creamed mixture to the yeast and flour mixture, and mix together, gradually drawing in the rest of the flour in the bowl.

4 Knead the dough well, then cover it and leave it to rest for 2–3 hours until doubled in size. Preheat the oven to 160°C/325°F/Gas 3.

5 Butter a Gugelhupf mould 25cm/10in in diameter, and dust it with flour. Fold the raisins with the brandy into the dough and turn it into the mould.

6 Bake for about 45 minutes, until golden brown. Leave to cool a little before turning the cake out of the mould. Cool on a wire rack and dust with icing sugar before serving.

Makes about 16 slices

100g/3½oz/¾ cup raisins
100ml/3½fl oz/scant ½ cup brandy
200ml/7fl oz/scant 1 cup milk
800g/1lb 6 oz/5½ cups plain (all-purpose) flour, plus extra for dusting
40g/1½oz fresh yeast
250g/9oz/generous 1 cup butter, softened
50g/2oz/¼ cup caster (superfine) sugar
½ tsp vanilla extract or 1 pack vanilla sugar (about 5g/2.5ml)
pinch of salt
8 eggs, lightly beaten
25ml/5 tsp baking powder
icing (confectioners') sugar, to dust

Cook's tip When baking with yeast every ingredient should be at room temperature to get the chemical reaction started. Take the eggs and butter out of the refrigerator in good time before you start the recipe.

Energy 371kcal/1556kJ; Protein 8.5g; Carbohydrate 47.1g, of which sugars 9g; Fat 16.4g, of which saturates 9.4g; Cholesterol 132mg; Calcium 106mg; Fibre 1.7g; Sodium 165mg

Makes about 12 slices

150g/5oz/10 tbsp butter, softened

150g/5oz/¾ cup caster (superfine) sugar

pinch of salt

5 eggs

15ml/1 tbsp almond liqueur

150g/5oz/1¼ cups plain (all-purpose) flour

50g/2oz/½ cup cornflour (cornstarch)

5ml/1 tsp baking powder

For the filling and topping

200g/7oz/1 cup caster sugar

6 egg yolks

20ml/4 tsp almond liqueur

200g/7oz/scant 1 cup butter, softened

100g/3½oz/1 cup chopped almonds

50g/2oz praline, finely chopped (see Cook's tip)

200g/7oz/⅔ cup red fruit jam (strawberry, cherry or redcurrant)

100ml/3½fl oz/scant ½ cup double (heavy) cream

12 glacé (candied) cherries

Cook's tip To make praline, oil a metal tray or marble slab. Heat 225g/8oz/1 cup caster (superfine) sugar in a heavy pan, swirling it until it melts and caramelizes. Stir in 115g/4oz/1 cup whole blanched almonds and pour immediately on to the oiled tray. Leave to cool then chop or smash. Stored in an airtight container. Praline can also be store-bought.

Warning The filling for this cake contains raw egg yolks, so is not suitable for infants, the elderly, pregnant women or convalescents.

Frankfurt crown cake
Frankfurter Kranz

My aunt used to make this cake and I loved it! I've tried a lot of other recipes but hers is the best, and I hope I have copied it faithfully. The cake is made in a similar way to the Black Forest gateau: first you bake a sponge cake, then you layer it with a cream filling.

1 Preheat the oven to 160°C/325°F/Gas 3 and butter a ring mould 25cm/10in in diameter. Cream the butter with the sugar, then beat in the salt, eggs and liqueur. Sift the flour, cornflour and baking powder and fold gently into the mixture. Turn into the mould and bake for about 45 minutes, until a skewer inserted in the centre comes out clean. Turn out on a wire rack and leave to cool.

2 For the filling and topping, beat the sugar with the egg yolks until light and thick, then beat in the liqueur. Whisk the butter until light and creamy, then slowly pour the egg and sugar mixture into the butter and beat it together.

3 Heat a frying pan over medium heat and toast the almonds for 2–3 minutes, stirring constantly, until they are golden. Leave to cool, then mix with the praline.

4 Slice the cake horizontally into three layers. Spread some of the cream filling on the first layer, then half the jam. Put the second layer of cake on top and repeat. Top with the last layer and spread the remaining filling all over the cake.

5 Sprinkle the almonds and praline all over the cake. Whip the cream until stiff and put it in a piping (pastry) bag with a star nozzle. Pipe 12 whirls around the top of the cake and decorate each one with a glacé cherry.

Energy 598kcal/2497kJ; Protein 7.9g; Carbohydrate 57.4g, of which sugars 43.8g; Fat 39.1g, of which saturates 20.2g; Cholesterol 258mg; Calcium 94mg; Fibre 1.1g; Sodium 264mg

Gingerbread
Lebkuchen

Gingerbread belongs to Christmas just as much as presents under the Christmas tree. It is flavoured with cloves, cinnamon, ginger, cardamom, allspice and nutmeg, which can now be bought as Lebkuchen mix.

1 Preheat the oven to 160°C/325°F/Gas 3 and line a 40x30cm/16x12in baking tray with baking parchment.

2 Heat a frying pan over medium heat and toast the hazelnuts, moving them around so that they brown evenly. Remove from the heat, cool, then chop finely.

3 Beat the sugar with the eggs until the mixture is light and thick. Stir in the melted butter, the honey and the chopped hazelnuts. Sift the flour with the baking powder and spice mix and fold into the mixture.

4 Pour the batter into the prepared tray. Bake in the preheated oven for about 45 minutes. Take it out and leave to cool in the tin before cutting into squares.

Energy 741kcal/3106kJ; Protein 14.1g; Carbohydrate 89.1g, of which sugars 45.4g; Fat 38.9g, of which saturates 11.5g; Cholesterol 144mg; Calcium 166mg; Fibre 3.8g; Sodium 171mg

Makes 30 squares

300g/11oz/scant 3 cups hazelnuts

300g/11oz/1½ cups soft brown sugar

5 eggs

150g/5oz/10 tbsp butter, melted

100g/3½oz/⅓ cup honey

500g/1¼lb/5 cups plain (all-purpose) flour

25ml/5 tsp baking powder

25g/1oz Lebkuchen spice mix

Cook's tip If you like, melt some chocolate and spread it over the gingerbread once it has cooled.

Makes 1 large loaf

45ml/3 tbsp oil for frying

2 onions, finely chopped

800g/1¾lb strong white bread flour

5ml/1 tsp sugar

40g/1½oz fresh yeast

salt and ground white pepper

flour, to dust

Cook's tip When you are ready to bake the bread, fill a metal container with water and place it in the oven with the bread. The steam this produces gives the bread a better crust.

Onion bread
Zwiebelbrot

This hearty loaf makes a good accompaniment for grilled fish or meat and is great as a base for a sandwich. If you want an even more flavourful variation, you can add garlic or fresh chopped herbs.

1 Heat the oil in a frying pan over medium heat and fry the onions for 3 minutes until transparent, then remove the pan from the heat and leave to cool.

2 Mix the flour with the sugar. Dissolve the yeast in 500ml/17fl oz/generous 2 cups lukewarm water and stir into the flour. Knead the dough for 5 minutes, then cover it and let it rest in a warm place for 20 minutes. Line a baking sheet with baking parchment and preheat the oven to 200°C/400°F/Gas 6.

3 Knead the onion with its oil, salt and pepper into the dough. Form a round loaf and put it on the baking sheet. Let it rest for 20–30 minutes until the dough has doubled in size, then put it in the oven and bake for about 1 hour. Leave the loaf to cool before cutting it.

Energy 3184kcal/13487kJ; Protein 80g; Carbohydrate 657.4g, of which sugars 38.6g; Fat 44.2g, of which saturates 5g; Cholesterol 0mg; Calcium 1222mg; Fibre 30.4g; Sodium 36mg

Sourdough rye bread
Roggen-Sauerteigbrot

Bread is an essential part of German food culture, and much of it is sourdough – naturally leavened by wild yeasts. You can use this recipe to make many variations, adding herbs, spices, onions, garlic and nuts.

1 Put all the ingredients for the starter in a bowl and mix to a soft paste using your fingertips. Cover the bowl with a damp dish towel and leave in a warm place for about 36 hours, stirring after 24 hours.

2 Blend the yeast for the dough with the lukewarm water, add to the starter and mix thoroughly. In a large bowl, mix the rye, wholemeal and white flours with the salt and make a well in the centre. Pour in the yeast liquid and gradually draw in the flour to make a smooth dough.

3 Knead the dough for 8–10 minutes on a floured surface until smooth and elastic. Place in an oiled bowl, cover with oiled clear film (plastic wrap) and leave in a warm place for 1–2 hours. Oil a 1kg/2¼lb loaf tin (pan) and dust with flour.

4 Knead the dough again for 3 minutes, then put it into the tin. It should not be more than three-quarters full so that there is enough space for the bread to rise. Cover with oiled clear film and leave in a warm place for 2–3 hours.

5 Preheat the oven to 240°C/475°F/Gas 9. Bake the bread for 10 minutes, then fill a metal dish with water and put it in the oven – this will give the loaf a nice crust. Lower the temperature to 160°C/325°F/Gas 3 and bake the bread for a further 45 minutes. Take it out of the tin and return it to the oven for another 20 minutes. The loaf is done when the crust is brown and the base sounds hollow when tapped.

Energy 2065kcal/8793kJ; Protein 59.8g; Carbohydrate 459.1g, of which sugars 5.4g; Fat 11.8g, of which saturates 1.7g; Cholesterol 0mg; Calcium 372mg; Fibre 56.2g; Sodium 3942mg

Makes 1 large loaf

For the sourdough starter

75g/3oz/¾ cup rye flour

80ml/3fl oz/⅓ cup warm water

pinch caraway seeds

For the dough

15g/½oz fresh yeast

315ml/11fl oz/1⅓ cups lukewarm water

275g/10oz/2½ cups rye flour

150g/5oz1¼ cups wholemeal (whole-wheat) bread flour

150g/5oz/1¼ cups unbleached strong white bread flour

10ml/2 tsp salt

Cook's tips This version of sourdough bread includes yeast but has a good sourdough flavour. Sourdough bread takes some time because it needs a 'starter', but you may be able to buy this from some wholefood stores or specialist suppliers.

Leave the loaf to cool for a couple of hours before slicing and serving. Although warm bread is very tempting, it is difficult to digest.

Caraway seed rolls
Kümmelbrot-seele

It is very common, especially in the southern part of Germany, to add whole or ground caraway seeds to bread dough, whether it's dark rye bread made with sourdough or white bread. This recipe comes from the area around Lake Constance in the far south. It is very simple, but so delicious! Try these rolls filled with sausages, cheese or ham.

1 Mix the flour with the salt and caraway seeds. Dissolve the yeast in 600ml/ 1 pint/2 ½ cups lukewarm water and stir it into the flour. Knead the dough for 5 minutes, then cover it and leave it to rest in a warm place for 1 hour.

2 Preheat the oven to 240°C/475°F/Gas 9. Knead the dough again and leave it to rest for another 20 minutes. Then turn it out on to a floured work surface and shape it into a sausage about 30cm/12in long.

3 Cut off pieces of the dough about 5cm/2in thick and roll each piece with your hands until it is a roll about 15–20cm/6–8in long.

4 Line a baking tray with baking parchment. Arrange the rolls on the tray and leave them to rest for 20–30 minutes. Then brush them with water and sprinkle some coarse sea salt on top.

5 Put the tray in the preheated oven. Bake for 10 minutes, then reduce the temperature to 160°C/325°F/Gas 3 and bake for another 10–15 minutes, until the rolls are golden brown and sound hollow when tapped on the base.

Energy 342kcal/1456kJ; Protein 9.5g; Carbohydrate 77.9g, of which sugars 1.5g; Fat 1.4g, of which saturates 0.2g; Cholesterol 0mg; Calcium 141mg; Fibre 3.1g; Sodium 1575mg

Makes 10 rolls

1kg/2¼lb/9 cups strong white bread flour, plus extra to dust

20g/¾oz/1 tbsp salt

5ml/1 tsp caraway seeds, or 2.5ml/ ½ tsp ground caraway seeds

40g/1½oz fresh yeast

coarse sea salt

Cook's tip Place a metal container full of water in the oven with the bread. The steam this produces gives the bread a better crust.

Useful addresses

Australia

German Bistro
(restaurant offfering traditional
German cuisine)
223 Flinders Street
Adelaide 5000
Tel : +61 8 8232 2082

Hofbräuhaus Melbourne
(authentic German restaurant)
18-24 Market Lane
Melbourne 3000
Tel: +61 3 9663 3361
www.hofbrauhaus.com.au

Taste Gourmet Grocer & Café
(supplier of German groceries)
73 Victoria Street
East Gosford 2250
Tel: +61 2 4324 2130
www.tastegourmet.com.au

Canada

European Speciality Importers
(supplier of German food
products)
220 Prior Street
Vancouver, British Columbia
V6A 2E5
Tel: +1 604 688 9528
http://www.bcgermanfood.com/

Mak European Delicatessen
1335 Lawrence Avenue East
Toronto,
Ontario M3A 1C6
Tel: +1 416 444 0719
www.makdeli.com

Sauter's Inn Restaurant
(traditional German restaurant)
109 Old Kingston Road
Ajax,
Ontario L1T 3A6
Tel: +1 905 427 6760
www.sautersinn.com

Vancouver Alpen Club
(rustic German restaurant)
4875 Victoria Drive
Vancouver,
British Columbia V5N 4P3
Tel: +1 604 874 3811
www.vancouveralpenclub.ca

New Zealand

Der Metz
(restaurant offering authentic
German cuisine and beer)
5-11 Averill Avenue
Kohimarama 1071
Tel: +64 9528 8012

Heck German Smallgoods
(German gourmet butchery)
2 Burnside Crescent
Christchurch 8053
Phone: +64 3357 8290
www.heck.co.nz

Tasty & Delicious
(supplier of German food
and groceries)
12 Inverness Road,
Browns Bay
North Shore City 0630
Tel: +64 9479 9622
www.finefoodoasis.com

United Kingdom

The Backhaus Shop
(supplier of traditional hand-
baked German goods)
175 Ashburnham Road
Ham, Richmond TW10 7NR
Tel: 020 8948 6040
www.backhaus.co.uk

**Essential Ingredient
Catering Ltd**
(caterers specializing in
German food)
79 Brudenell Road
London SW17 8DD
Tel: 020 8767 6178
www.essentialingredient.co.uk

German Deli Shop
(supplies wide range of
imported German food and
delicatessen groceries)
127 Central Street
London EC1V 8AP
Tel: 020 7250 3322
www.germandeli.co.uk

**Kurz & Lang – The Bratwurst
Company**
(Bratwurst specialist)
1 St John Street
London EC1M 4AA
Tel: 020 7253 6623
www.kurzandlang.com

United States

Café Berlin
323 14th Street
Denver,
Colorado 80202
Tel: +1 303 377 5896
www.cafeberlindenver.com

**Esther's German Bakery
and Cafe**
987 N. San Antonio Road
Los Altos,
California 94022
Tel: +1 650 941 4463
www.esthersbakery.com

GermanDeli.com
(online supermarket)
P.O. Box 92773
Southlake,
Texas 76092
Tel: +1 877 437 6269

GermanFoodSpecialties.com
(online supermarket)
14700 Dade Pine Avenue
Miami Lakes,
Florida 33014
Tel: +1 305 362 1923

Jasper Strassenfest
On the streets of Jasper,
Indiana, an annual
festival in August is held to
celebrate German heritage
and culture
www.jasperstrassenfest.org

Zum Rheingarten Restaurant
(traditional German restaurant)
3998 Jefferson Davis Highway
Stafford,
Virginia 22554
Tel: +1 703 221 4635
www.zumrheingarten.com

Index

A
apples 8, 15
  apple and potato mash
    with black pudding 47
  apple fritters with fruits in
rum 99
  apple strudel with vanilla
sauce 101
  baked apples with
    marzipan 102
  carrot and apple cream
    soup 32
  Nuremberg sausages with
    apple sauerkraut 46
  poor knights with apples 98
asparagus 16
  asparagus and smoked fish
salad 24
  asparagus soup with North
    Sea prawns 33

B
bacon
  matjes herring with bacon
and onions 53
  pears, beans and bacon 73
  sauerkraut soup with
    bacon 35
barley 8
Bavarian cream with berries 103
Bavarian platter 40
beans 10
  pears, beans and bacon 73
beef 15
  beef with beetroot,
    potatoes and herring 62
  beef with raisin sauce and
    dumplings 67
  calves' liver Berlin-style 68
  simmered beef topside with
horseradish 63
  Swabian beef stew with
    spätzle 64
  veal meatballs in white
    caper sauce 69
beer 6, 9, 10, 11, 17
beetroot 16
  beef with beetroot,
    potatoes and herring 62

berries 15
  Bavarian cream with berries
    103
Black Forest gateau 113
black pudding
  apple and potato mash
    with black pudding 47
boar with sprouts and
  poached pears 90
brassicas 16
bread 6, 7, 12, 17
  caraway seed rolls 124
  onion bread 121
  poor knights with apples 98
  sourdough rye bread 123
Brussels sprouts 16
  wild boar with sprouts and
    poached pears 90
butter 6
butter cake with caramelized
almonds 110

C
cabbage 8, 11, 16
  cabbage stuffed with pork
    72
  duck legs with red cabbage
    88
  pork with cabbage
    and bread dumplings 76
  red cabbage salad with
    walnuts 22
  roast duck with cabbage
and potatoes 85
calves' liver Berlin-style 68
capers
  veal meatballs in white
    caper sauce 69

caraway 17
  caraway seed rolls 124
carrots 16
  carrot and apple cream
    soup 32
catfish
  fried catfish with cucumber
    salad 54
cheese 6–7, 10, 12, 15
  Bavarian platter 40
  German cheesecake with
raisins 108
  Rhenish sausage salad with
Emmental 28
  spätzle with cheese and
onions 43
chicken 15
  chicken fricassée 82
  chicken in Riesling with
    roast potatoes 83
chocolate
  Black Forest gateau 113
Christmas 11
coffee 12, 17
condiments 17
crayfish
  perfect spring vegetables
with crayfish 41
cream 15
  Bavarian cream with berries
    103
  carrot and apple cream
    soup 32
cucumber
  fried catfish with cucumber
    salad 54

D
dairy products 6–7, 9, 15
drinks 17
duck 11, 13, 15
  duck with red cabbage 88
  roast duck with cabbage
and potatoes 85
dumplings 10, 11
  beef with raisin sauce and
    dumplings 67
  pork with cabbage
    and bread dumplings 76

E
Easter 10
eel 14
  scrambled eggs with
    prawns and smoked
      eel 45
eggs 12
  scrambled eggs with
    prawns and smoked eel
      45

F
fish 7, 8, 9, 10, 12, 14
  asparagus and smoked
    fish salad 24
  fish fillets in creamy
    mustard sauce 56
flavourings 17
Frankfurt crown cake 118
fruit 9, 15–16
  red fruit jelly Hamburg-style
    96

G
game 7, 8
German cheesecake with
  raisins 108
German ring cake 117
Germany 6–7
  classic ingredients
    14–17
  festivals and celebrations
    10–11
  food traditions 12–13
  geography 8–9
gherkins 17
gingerbread 13, 120

goose 11, 13, 15
    roast goose with chestnut
        stuffing 86

H
ham 12, 14–15
    parsnip soup with Black
Forest ham 31
herbs 6, 17
herring 14
    matjes herring with bacon
and onions 53
    tartare of matjes herring
        and salmon 27
horseradish 6, 17
    simmered beef topside with
horseradish 63

J
juniper berries 6, 15

L
lamb 10, 13, 15
    braised lamb with potatoes
        70

M
marzipan with baked apples
    102
meat 6, 7, 12, 14–15
milk 6–7, 15
mushrooms 16–17
mussels with root vegetables
    57
mustard 6, 15, 17
    fish fillets in creamy
        mustard sauce 56

N
New Year's Eve 10
Nuremberg sausages with
    apple sauerkraut 46

nuts 11
    butter cake with
caramelized almonds 110
    red cabbage salad with
        walnuts 22
    roast goose with chestnut
        stuffing 86

O
obatza 40
October 3 11
onions
    matjes herring with bacon
and onions 53
    onion bread 121
    spätzle with cheese and
onions 43

P
parsnip soup with Black
    Forest ham 31
pears
    pears, beans and bacon 73
    wild boar with sprouts
        and poached pears 90
plum cake streusel 111
pork 6, 13, 14
    cabbage stuffed with pork
        72
    pork in aspic with
        remoulade sauce 75
    pork with cabbage and bread
        dumplings 76
    wild boar with sprouts and
        poached pears 90
potatoes 7, 8, 10, 16
    apple and potato mash
        with black pudding 47
    beef with beetroot, potatoes
        and herring 62
    braised lamb with potatoes
        70
    chicken in Riesling with
        roast potatoes 83
    potato pancakes with
        smoked salmon 44
    potato salad with
        frankfurters 10, 30
    potato soup with sausages
        34
    roast duck with cabbage
        and potatoes 85
    venison goulash with potato
        cakes 89

poultry 7
    asparagus soup with North
Sea prawns 33
    scrambled eggs with
        prawns and smoked
        eel 45
pumpkin 16
    spiced pickled pumpkin 23

R
raisins
    beef with raisin sauce and
        dumplings 67
    German cheesecake with
        raisins 108
remoulade sauce 75
Rhenish mussels with root
vegetables 57
Rhenish sausage salad with
Emmental 28
Riesling 6, 17
    chicken in Riesling with
        roast potatoes 83
rumtopf 15–16
    apple fritters with fruits in
        rum 99
rye bread 6, 14, 15
    sourdough rye bread 123

S
salmon 14
    potato pancakes with
        smoked salmon 44
    tartare of matjes herring
        and salmon 27
sauerkraut 6, 13, 17
    Nuremberg sausages with
        apple sauerkraut 46
    sauerkraut soup with bacon
        35
sausages 6, 7, 12, 13, 14, 17
    Bavarian platter 40

Nuremberg sausages with
    apple sauerkraut 46
potato salad with
    frankfurters 10, 30
potato soup with sausages
    34
Rhenish sausage salad with
    Emmental 28
semolina flummery with
    strawberries 97
spätzle
    spätzle with cheese and
        onions 43
    Swabian beef stew with
        spätzle 64
spices 6, 12, 17
spirits 17
spring carnivals 10
St Nicholas 11
stollen 13, 114
strawberries 15
    semolina flummery with
        strawberries 97
streusel plum cake 111
summer festivals 11
Swabian beef stew with
    spätzle 64

T
tea 12, 17
trout 9, 14
    Fried trout, miller's wife-style 52

V
vanilla
    apple strudel with vanilla
        sauce 101
veal meatballs in white caper
    sauce 69
vegetables 6, 7, 8, 9, 16–17
    perfect spring vegetables
        with crayfish 41
    Rhenish mussels with root
        vegetables 57
venison 11, 15
    venison goulash 89

W
wheat 8
wine 6, 11, 13, 17
    chicken in Riesling with
        roast potatoes 83